D0458801

Ballard Branch

Praise for *All for Love*

"This wise, heartfelt book guides us in creating a loving space for ourselves and others in an increasingly divided and volatile world."

Tara Brach
author of *Trusting the Gold*

"A practical blueprint that takes you on an enriching journey to achieve unconditional love through heartfelt communication, while healing our past wounds and eliminating conflict. You will experience rewarding relationships that lead to joy and fulfillment in every area of your life. A must-read."

Anita Moorjani
New York Times bestselling author of *Dying to Be Me*, *What If This Is Heaven?*, and *Sensitive Is the New Strong*

"The wisdom, insights, and practices within this book not only hold the key to personal transformation, but they also hold the key to a brighter, more compassionate, and more sincere world. Every reader who engages with this book will be changed, and that change has no choice but to show up in this world in the most beautifully empowered and intentional way. What a blessing!"

Kerri Walsh Jennings
three-time gold and one-time bronze Olympic medalist on the US beach volleyball team

All for Love

ALSO BY MATT KAHN

*Whatever Arises, Love That: A Love
Revolution That Begins with You*

*Everything Is Here to Help You: A Loving
Guide to Your Soul's Evolution*

*The Universe Always Has a Plan: The 10
Golden Rules of Letting Go*

MATT KAHN

All for Love

The **Transformative Power** of **Holding Space**

sounds true
BOULDER, COLORADO

Sounds True
Boulder, CO 80306

Published 2022

Book design by Linsey Dodaro

The wood used to produce this book is from Forest
Stewardship Council (FSC) certified forests, recycled
materials, or controlled wood.

Printed in Canada

BK06385

Library of Congress Cataloging-in-Publication Data

Names: Kahn, Matt, author.
Title: All for love : the transformative power of holding space /
    Matt Kahn.
Description: Boulder, CO : Sounds True, 2022.
Identifiers: LCCN 2021039911 (print) | LCCN 2021039912 (ebook) |
    ISBN 9781683649144 (hardcover) | ISBN 9781683649151 (ebook)
Subjects: LCSH: Interpersonal communication. | Self-realization. |
    Resilience (Personality trait)
Classification: LCC BF637.C45 K33 2022 (print) | LCC BF637.C45
    (ebook) | DDC 158.1--dc23
LC record available at https://lccn.loc.gov/2021039911
LC ebook record available at https://lccn.loc.gov/2021039912

10 9 8 7 6 5 4 3 2 1

TO JULIE DITTMAR:

Your friendship is one of the greatest gifts I've ever received. Thank you for this journey and for the brand new chapter we've entered.

CONTENTS

INTRODUCTION   1

CHAPTER 1   Being Helpful Begins with Listening   7

CHAPTER 2   It's Not a Matter of What
                 Anyone Else *Doesn't* Know   25

CHAPTER 3   You Can't Rush What Has
                 Been Buried for So Long   41

CHAPTER 4   Anger Is a Reenactment
                 of Someone Else's Trauma   53

CHAPTER 5   When Someone Fights Their
                 Pain, You Get Pushed Away   69

CHAPTER 6   Diversity Is the Guiding
                 Light of Compassion   87

CHAPTER 7   Boundaries Are an
                 Act of Self-Love   101

CHAPTER 8   Gratitude Is Always
                 Appropriate   113

CHAPTER 9   Facing "What Is" Can Be
                 Uncomfortable, and That's Okay   127

CHAPTER 10   Time Is the Wisest Healer   141

CONCLUSION   157

Acknowledgments   159

About the Author   161

Introduction

As a marker for this exact point in history, I sit here in front of my computer in a world still adjusting to mask wearing and social distancing, reeling from generations of racial divide, and staggered by a violent attack on our nation's capital. Whether separated by race, culture, gender, sexual orientation, identity preference, or opinion, it seems the many cracks spread throughout our world have only widened into deeper gaps of social conflict.

While many believe our evolution as a species has placed us at the brink of despair, I see this as a golden opportunity to awaken our consciousness on the largest scale possible. Maybe it's the wake-up call this world never knew it needed. What if the current conflicts are actually openings to explore true peace and unity with our fellow human beings? What if, as a way to shift toward a more conscious, compassionate, and interconnected society, we are becoming more aware of the pain that separates each heart from the sum of the whole. Perhaps this is how humanity evolves into the Aquarian Age of collective heart expansion—unlike at any other time in recorded history.

As a signpost for these times, each difference we sense in others can become a profound invitation to explore a greater depth of interconnectedness. Instead of spirituality being a topic we quietly discuss in private, the importance of its role in uniting the world continues to spread rapidly across every continent. Of course, with any opportunity for individual and collective growth comes the need for a skill set to help us navigate that trajectory. In order to birth an evolutionary species that's willing to be better than any generation before it, we must be willing to reach within our hearts and give to one another the respect, validation, and encouragement we all deserve and desire. If the destiny of our species is to be more conscious and compassionate, then the skills we are inspired to implement on a daily basis must be equally rooted in the same principles. In that way, we will become the tangible change each of us wishes to see. This is why you are here receiving the gifts that living All For Love has to offer.

The Transformative Power of Holding Space

Perhaps you are asking yourself, *What does holding space actually mean for me and for others?* In her UPLIFT article "What It Means to Hold Space for Someone," author and teacher Heather Plett says that holding space "means we are willing to walk alongside another person in whatever journey they're on without judging them, making them feel inadequate, trying to fix them, or trying to impact the outcome. When we hold space for other people, we open our hearts, offer unconditional support, and let go of judgement and control."

Rheeda Walker, a clinical psychologist, researcher, and professor at the University of Houston and the author of *The Unapologetic Guide to Black Mental Health* offers a complementary explanation: "Holding space . . . means taking the initiative, without any prompting, to be empathic to another person's situation or circumstance and making time for that individual to do whatever is needed for them, like voicing hurt, anger, or another strong emotion and receiving whatever they need to communicate in a way that is supportive and nonjudgmental."

The importance of space holding begins with an awareness that all human beings are on journey of existential growth and emotional maturity. Because every living form is a manifestation of consciousness, each is interconnected with a source of loving divine intelligence whose nature is to constantly evolve, grow, and expand. This is why each moment has been designed to place you into situations and guide you through circumstances that help you move from one level of consciousness to the next. While it is the will of each person to decide how often they choose to evolve, the gift of inspired heartfelt support fuels profound healing and furthers the most triumphant breakthroughs in all of us.

When you genuinely offer yourself or others the gift of support, this kindness sends the message that while we are all navigating our own paths, no one is ever as alone as they may feel—especially when they know how to meet conflict with a peaceful, loving response. Because moments of interaction always serve the progress of our highest evolution, each encounter also provides countless opportunities to strengthen bonds of intimacy, whether the results unfold as planned, or they have inspired the stress of unexpected change. The more we learn how to hold space for the transformation of growth expanding within ourselves, the easier it will be to face any difficulty, even when others react from their most insufferable judgments, pain, and fear.

As an incredible resource for your journey, I have written *All for Love: The Transformative Power of Holding Space* to help resolve moments of conflict with the practical wisdom of conscious communication to assist everyone—especially emotionally sensitive empathic beings—to embrace their ever-changing world with bravery, confidence, and compassion.

Throughout this book, I detail ten principles to help you transform the difficulties of human interaction into a sacred space of intimate connection. Chapter by chapter, each principle will help you cultivate a specific attribute that will maximize your opportunity to respond with mindfulness rather than letting emotionally fueled reactions speak on your behalf. I also share stories from my own life to shed light on how this heart-centered way of communication found its way to me and now into the beauty of your experience. In each chapter, I offer key supportive statements that will help you embody the sharing of each principle and contribute to the benefit of your evolution, those you love, and our ever-changing world.

It is important to keep in mind that mastering the art of holding space is much like a yoga practice. You can't simply move your body into a position and expect to achieve perfection on your first try. You have to slowly find your way into a posture and even modify it to suit your needs, strengths, and weaknesses. Much is the same with holding space, so please always be gentle with yourself.

Through a willingness to lower your emotional shields, surrender each weapon of verbal defense, and begin exploring reality from a new paradigm of perception, I am honored to supply you with the insights, opportunities to heal, and necessary tools to resolve the conflicts that may surface along the way.

As we acknowledge how much more we can learn by bringing together our individual perspectives, we inspire each other to become the generations that helped turn an unsustainable way of living toward a more hopeful and conscious future.

And So We Begin . . .

May the words you are about to read offer you everything you need to answer the timeless question: When life gets overwhelming, and I don't know what to do, what do I say to myself and to those around me?

May the ten principles, attributes, and supportive statements in *All for Love* inspire more encouraging self-talk instead of painful inner criticism.

May they help you learn how to be a better friend to the wounds hiding inside your heart and lurking in the shadows of people you know.

May they help you make peace with hurtful memories, forgive those who truly couldn't have done any better, and teach you how to navigate a path of serenity no matter how others around you behave.

May they deepen the intimacy of your relationships and help you feel more engaged in life, allowing you to open up and let your voice be heard.

May they help you feel more supported by learning how to best support others without giving away all of your time and energy.

May they release you from the grip of perfectionism, codependency, and people pleasing as you reclaim the personal power you wholeheartedly deserve.

May they help you become more naturally immune to the unconscious activities of those who may view you as a new place to hide from pain.

Best of all, may they help you become so aware of the differences between your experiences and others around you that you are able to make empowering choices from a position of freedom without getting lost in the intensity of someone else's patterning.

From my heart to yours, thank you for exploring a road less traveled, as a gift of evolution for yourself, those you love, all who came before you, and all who may ever come to be.

Thank you for exploring the transformative power of holding space at a critical moment when space is needed to be held for the exquisite unfoldment of our rebirthing humanity.

All for light, all for life, all for love,
Matt Kahn

CHAPTER 1

Being Helpful Begins
with Listening

Before most of my spiritual experiences occurred, I was an emotionally sensitive, empathic child who had misinterpreted others' emotional experiences as the negative opinions I believed they had of me. To complicate my life even more, I had an open mind, an infinite number of questions, and a very short attention span. When you combine the excitement of inner curiosity with an inability to give anything your complete focus, you can be caught in a rather ungrounded spiral. Just as this blend of forces may lead to exploring spiritual wisdom without an ability to truly absorb it, in my earliest relationships, I was excited to make friends but had no way to be present with the kids I was so eager to meet. I remember wanting to know the lives of so many new faces I saw running around the schoolyard. I would introduce myself with the best of intentions and then experience an equal degree of agony when the words the other kids shared were longer than the short bursts of ideas I could absorb.

As an adult, I can reflect on my earlier years with greater clarity. I was raised in a household of codependency and functional alcoholism. My parents were simultaneously wise, loving, my greatest supporters, and emotionally volatile. I remember learning to wince, contract, and shut down at their sheer tone and volume. Especially if I heard "Matthew!" instead of "Matt," I knew an interrogation was coming my way. This also created a hypervigilance in me. From a codependent standpoint, I grew to fear my power since my self-expression seemed to trigger my parents, leading me to believe that my very existence could cause someone pain.

From an adult mindset, I can see how my mom and dad were my earliest models of the "outside world." Because of their outbursts, I developed a fear of other people, a fear of my mere presence hurting them, and a fear of the ways they could suddenly turn on me. To protect myself, I learned to shut down and tune out my parents' explosive tirades. This also became the way my short attention span would tune out others when they spoke at greater lengths. Because my parents could quickly switch between the emotional extremes of lovingkindness and anger, I subconsciously developed a pattern of mentally drifting off if anyone shared deeply. I would anticipate the inevitable flip I'd experienced in my household as the judgments, rejection, blame, and emotional abandonment I was prepared to endure. This is why, in hindsight, my tendency to check out was never a matter of not caring about others. It was more an inability to feel safe when listening due to the unpredictable volatility of my household.

But as I grew, I became increasingly aware of how deeply I wanted other people to know the innocence hiding within my shutdown human shell. Eventually, I was able to notice how open and interested others were when I took a sincere interest in them. It required bravery and a willingness to listen and to face the possibility of misunderstanding and disapproval I'd spent a large part of my life fearing.

With each and every attempt to listen to others, I began to glimpse moments of relief. Even for just a split second, I would see so clearly how the very act of listening could be relaxing rather than contracting. I also recognized that it was impossible to listen authentically while fearing disapproval. I began to learn that the more I enjoyed getting to know the uniqueness of others, the more ease and the less fear I sensed. This gave them the chance to know and embrace me. While it would take many years to piece this all together, at the time, I was intrigued by one defining insight: the deeper I listened, the less frightened I became.

My new awareness even led my mom to ask me on many occasions, "What's wrong with you, Matthew? You've become so quiet." At those times, she would gently press the back of her hand to my forehead to check if I had a fever. What she hadn't realized, and what I couldn't yet articulate, was how safe, comfortable, and fulfilled I now felt during the act of listening. What once seemed like impatient agony or the nearly paralyzing fear of being judged and persecuted now became an engaging way to observe the individuality of others. I even found that if I listened deeply when my parents would react, I could stay within my safe, relaxed bubble of curiosity and not feel whipped around by their emotional blowouts.

As this occurred, I also noticed there were different levels of listening. The first was one of agreement: Do I agree with what they're saying? Do I agree with how they're seeing me? Do I agree with their opinions, beliefs, or viewpoints? Such questions helped me recognize that when I disagreed with others, I would stop listening to them as a protest against their ideas and projections. But as soon as I did this, a familiar lack of safety swiftly returned. Now, my only recourse was to people please and beg for forgiveness for whatever I believed I did wrong to clear the emotional weight I was carrying for them.

Whether or not I approved of anyone's viewpoint, I discovered a second, deeper level of listening. Instead of judging other people's perspectives, I began to see how their experiences were mainly shaped by the unprocessed pain they carried within. While it would take years to make sense of this, I had a rapidly growing awareness that made others' opinions less about their perceptions of me and more about the emotional conflicts brewing within them.

From this deeper understanding, I was able to see two distinctive sides to my parents: When they were open, everything they shared was wise, supportive, and helpful. Once they were upset, much of what they said felt mean-spirited, one-sided, and out of sync with reality. When my parents would act this way, I sensed it wasn't their innocent nature doing the damage but the vices and patterns that robbed them of their power.

Learning how to listen without needing to adopt or criticize someone else's perspective helped free me of the emotional complications I could feel in others. With more time spent letting others be seen and heard, this skill naturally evolved into a third, more engaging level of listening that I often refer to as encouragement.

The Attribute of Encouragement

As the first attribute in the space-holding process, encouragement is a form of dynamic listening. It's dynamic in the sense that you don't just hear the ideas others wish to share from a passive, submissive standpoint. Rather, you take an active role in honoring the journey they're on—a journey that will likely differ from the choices, perceptions, interests, ambitions, and insights that resonate with you.

In the attribute of encouragement, you aren't trying to change how anyone thinks. Neither are you working to sway them toward your perspective. Nor do you believe that by hearing their testimony of life, you are less rooted in your own truth. This may help you remember how the act of listening doesn't make you a part of someone else's narrative. As a dynamic listener, the attribute of encouragement allows you to authentically support others without needing to always find common ground. You might say, for instance, "I hear you." Or, "Thanks for sharing your point of view with me." Or, "We will get through this together." These are ways to convey encouraging support without having to blindly agree with other people's perspectives.

There may be times when others' thoughts, hopes, and desires are far removed from your own view of reality. But because encouragement is a facet of consciousness, your dynamic listening will help expand their awareness just by supporting their path—a path that may ultimately lead them to an inevitable moment of clarity, no matter how out of balance they may seem to you right now.

In the beginning stages of interpersonal communication, you are likely to find great purpose when sharing with people who wholeheartedly agree with you—your friends, family, or people of similar spiritual interests or political affiliations. In fact, you'll probably derive fleeting bursts of joy from the many perspectives, beliefs, and ideas you have in common. But when connecting with like-minded people becomes a necessity rather than a choice, it can narrow the true fulfillment of interactions as it leads you to believe that conversations are only pleasurable when everyone agrees.

As your consciousness expands, you'll find that you are not just satisfied by mutual agreements with others who think, speak, act, or choose as you do. Through the attribute of encouragement, you will set aside the necessity of common ground by daring to support the uniqueness of someone else's journey as it simultaneously supports your own evolution. Because reality is governed by the spiritual law of unity consciousness, the more encouraging you are in the lives of others, the more you will feel encouraged, even when someone else can't meet you as you wish to be met.

The attribute of encouragement not only opens the door for greater emotional connection, but it also frees you from believing that your role is to correct the course of others who, in your opinion, appear to be misguided or misinformed.

Some people may read this and believe that it is inauthentic to support the choices of others if they differ from their own. While any conversation is a dance of sharing and listening, the controlling viewpoint, "If I were you, I'd choose differently," rarely goes over well. This unconscious tendency is likely to create more conflict, especially if it causes you to believe you are less connected to your inner truth when others share different perspectives.

Whenever two people speak without listening to each other, it can spark a battle for control. This is because the differences in your choices and perceptions are what make you—uniquely you. Equally so, other people's choices and opinions are just as valid for their evolution. No matter how we behave, each of us is always being guided along our own path into higher levels of awareness and maturity. Despite the different versions of others you may wish to engage, you cannot control how anyone's destiny unfolds. Instead, you are witnessing how much you are able to evolve when supporting the journey someone is on.

Through the attribute of encouragement, transformation can naturally arise for everyone involved since the benefit of healing relies on the simple act of being heard. This is why throughout the process of holding space, you will come to learn how being helpful always begins with listening.

Of course, if you notice abusive actions or hear someone confess to their participation in unlawful activity, you have now become a witness to criminal behavior. As a citizen of the world, it's your right and duty to report this to local authorities. But since these circumstances are rare, the majority of sharing you will hear is likely to involve the regrets, concerns, and confusion of unprocessed pain. The more openly you are able to listen, the more often you will find that your ability to lead with encouragement unfolds naturally. This allows you to sense the palpable depth of your own safety when empathizing with other people's experiences rather than only listening on the surface level of agreement.

From a space-holding standpoint, instead of forming an opinion about what people say, feel into their words on a deeper level. This will help you tune in to the uniqueness of their journey from a more heart-centered perspective. You may ask yourself, *What must this person be feeling or have endured to think, speak, or act this way?* From this question of empathy, the power of your interest can more openly offer blessings of encouragement to their heart—no matter what differences divide you. This becomes a huge step toward emotional freedom, as you dare to be a supporter of someone's journey, even if they act unsupportively toward you. Contrary to popular opinion, you may not actually feel disappointed by their lack of support. Instead, you will begin to see so clearly how disappointment mainly occurs when you withhold your greatest support from those unwilling to meet you openly.

Why can't people meet you as you are? Because they're hurting. Why can't you always be the idealized version of yourself? Because you are hurting as well.

The sooner you realize that disappointment is often caused by withholding kindness toward others in pain, the easier it is to be open—no matter how closed off or shut down someone seems to be.

Human interactions are an expression of free will. When a person wants to share, they often ask, "Can I have a moment of your time?" What they're really asking is "Are you in a space to listen and encourage, no matter what I am ready to share?" From this more aware perspective, conflict occurs for those who are more interested in proving their points than listening. Equally so, you can invite greater peace into each interaction when listening and encouraging become your primary response.

As it's cultivated, you will come to see how the attribute of encouragement is not just a matter of mindlessly placating someone's subjective experiences. Rather, it's one of the most heart-centered ways to consciously engage for everyone's evolutionary benefit:

> By encouraging others, may you feel more encouraged throughout your own life.

> By listening to others beyond simple agreement, may you equally develop the space to hear the voice of your own needs, even when it seems as if no one but you cares to listen.

> May you uncover your true wholeness and vitality when fueled by the generosity of giving, regardless of how it's interpreted or received.

What Could Possibly Go Wrong?

While most people aim to be prepared with the precise instructions of a new skill set, hoping to guarantee an end result that increases their comfort and minimizes discord, life often doesn't work that way along the learning curve of conscious communication. By confronting each growth-inducing scenario of possibility, you can learn to engage with life and the people around you in the most open and dynamic way. This also encourages you to step outside your comfort zone to refine your space-holding process through the grace and bravery of practical application.

Along the way, you will have successes, resets, and a few epic, hall-of-fame-worthy blunders just to keep your feet firmly grounded on Earth. In addressing what could possibly go wrong in this chapter and throughout the book, it's my intention to help you overcome any fear of failure, freeing you from trying to do things so correctly that you overlook the joy and exhilaration of exploring your journey on life's unpredictable terms.

It's true. Life can be totally unpredictable despite your best intentions. People can be really unfair. How unfair? Here are a few examples:

- With the most radiantly open heart, you may reach out to someone only to be met by a response that has more to do with their hurtful past than a new opportunity of connection that you represent in the present.

- You might be blamed for causing someone to revisit painful memories, all because your interest in their experience didn't create a new hiding spot for elusive patterns of avoidance.

- Someone might lash out at you for taking a greater interest in their experiences because it interrupts their inner narrative of rejection, inferiority, self-pity, and entitlement.

- You might encourage someone whom you quickly realize insists on arguing with anyone in sight, just so they can bypass bringing their greater vulnerabilities into full awareness.

No matter what results you elicit, whether you're pleasantly surprised by the deeper connections or mesmerized by the reactions of others—isn't that okay?

It's totally normal and natural to not ace it each time. It's even fine to be an incredible space holder even when you're the only person to recognize your growth. Undoubtedly, we incarnated onto the Earth plane to learn, and there isn't one person walking the face of this planet who is done growing.

The important thing to remember is this: you are developing a set of skills that ensures that no matter how anyone reacts to you or comes or goes in your life, you will continually step into your power by being your biggest supporter and responding with compassion rather than fueling conflict by lashing out or shutting down. As holding space replaces the patterning of reactions, you can remain connected to yourself, despite how disconnected you may feel from others. You can rest in the certainty of your own unwavering support to carry you through even the most uncertain times. Slowly but surely, you will become such an ally for your own evolving journey that the fear of the unknown will transform into an excitement to go where your awareness has never gone before. From this space, you will see the disappointing actions of humanity as the unconscionable results of unprocessed pain begging for the acceptance, forgiveness, and love it doesn't know how to trust or actually receive.

Sometimes encouragement will feel like a superpower. At other times, it will feel like a black plague spreading wildly in an environment of unhappy people. The very word en*courage*ment reminds you of the courage required to support someone who may have had so little experience feeling supported, they may not know how to let in your kindness. Ultimately, that's the nature of their journey. Let it be their choice to decide if, how, and when they receive the gifts you offer. Your journey is simply to determine the depth and frequency of your giving.

Most importantly, regardless of the reactions of others, the encouragement they may or may not know how to receive can always become the very gift of greater support you can offer yourself when it matters most. When others deny or dismiss the support you give, most likely they are too paralyzed in trauma response to initially perceive your generosity as anything but a threat based on their orbiting collection of memories. That's okay too. Congratulate yourself. You tried. You gave someone a gift that planted seeds for the beauty of future growth. Sometimes you will even attract experiences meant to go wrong, just to help you face and move beyond the fear of failure, so you'll be able to offer encouragement with more openness, authenticity, and ease the next time around. As crazy as it sounds, life orchestrates a symphony of chaos and helps you manifest a mixed bag of results just so you can say to yourself, *Wow. That went horribly wrong. It wasn't what I expected or intended, but somehow, I'm still whole,* and ultimately discover for yourself, *It's okay that others aren't able to receive what I'm able to give. It helps me notice the differences in our experiences. We don't actually need to find common ground. All that is required is for me to be open.*

This also means you don't always have to explore interpersonal pain in order to connect. Not every conversation has to be a dumpster dive into life's most harrowing memories. Interactions don't always require emotional processing in order to be meaningful. Equally so, someone else's off day, bad mood, or unrelenting circumstances don't have to shut down your support or destroy your experience when you're honoring their reality with heartfelt encouragement.

With each attempt, your success becomes more dependent on the purity of your contribution—all so that you can be firmly rooted in the fulfillment of giving instead of waiting to receive what others may not be ready to provide.

Setting an Intention for Encouragement

To release attachments to outcome and hold encouraging space for yourself and others, please repeat the following words out loud:

> I intend to hold space through the attribute of encouragement for myself and others without attachment to outcome. I allow my encouragement to be agenda free, as an offering of compassionate support for the healing of all. I recognize that each person is navigating the trajectory of their unique journey and can only perceive me, interpret my actions, and receive my gifts in whatever way they can. Because I mindfully act from a heart-centered space that respects the journey

they're on, I do not intend to interfere with their process but to simply offer the gift of loving support.

I allow any encouragement I offer to be received, rejected, denied, or interpreted in any way that supports the well-being of whomever I meet. If and when this hurts my feelings, triggers memories of past traumas, makes me more distrustful of others, or causes me to shut down in rejection or lash out in resentment, I allow myself the sacred space to be with my feelings and offer the gift of encouragement to any part of me. I honor the attribute of encouragement as a way of reminding others of their true worth and value and to let them know they're never alone despite how isolated, rejected, or heartbroken they may feel. Whether given to myself or another person or as an active blessing to humanity, I welcome and allow the attribute of encouragement to show me a renewed depth of fulfillment that comes from the grace of giving, instead of the expectations I may have toward others. And so it is.

The Supportive Statement of Encouragement

"I Would Love to Hear More about the Events That Led to Your Feelings"

When listening through the attribute of encouragement, you are open to knowing more about the details and circumstances that shape each person's experience. While someone's cultural up-bringing and history may differ from yours, the emotions each person carries within themselves and might be afraid to face are those that you too have felt and may have internalized. As the attribute of encouragement invites others to feel safe enough to share, it also helps you process your own unresolved traumas, just by taking a greater, more compassionate interest in the experiences they're having.

Since many people project the residue of unbearable memories onto their current reality, they often assume new experiences will more than likely be echoes of a painful past. As a result, they are left without the courage or curiosity to welcome a different outcome. This is why one of the prime objectives of holding space is to lovingly invite someone to be vulnerable with whatever depth of encouragement you are willing to convey.

You can offer this kind of encouragement just by suggesting, "I would love to hear more about the events that led to your feelings." This supportive statement can also be applied to your own healing. In my first book, *Whatever Arises, Love That,* I detail the process of connecting with your inner child to heal the wounds of your heart. This helps you move out of the identity of your earliest pain to recognize in yourself the parent, friend, guardian, and companion you always wanted and needed. In order to connect with your inner child, it's essential to know what to say. This is where a statement such as "I would love to hear more about the events that led to your feelings" can invite deeper sharing from the parts in you waiting to be seen and heard.

If you seek to correct instead of connect with your inner child, you are meeting it like an unsolicited life coach rather than its greatest supporter. This can create greater distrust and discord with the parts that just want to know if it's safe to come out of hiding. One of the most direct ways you can convey such safety is through the interest only you can authentically provide. Prior to stepping out of the shadows of pain and into the light of your consciousness, your inner child needs to know it's allowed to share any feeling without being corrected, shamed, punished, rejected, or abandoned as it may so vividly remember from previous experiences. While the events you survived may not be new information to process, it's crucial to allow your inner child to share, providing you the chance to revisit difficult memories from your more aware adult perspective.

Even when the statement "I would love to hear more about the events that led to your feelings" is met with silence, it simply indicates that your inner child is still building trust with you. While it may seem unwilling to engage, it silently awaits more consistent interactions to know you're safer, more trustworthy, and more reliable than any hurtful past. No matter how resistant it may feel, the gift of your encouragement is all it ever needs.

This is also true when interacting with others. They may rightfully withhold grim details from the painful events that lead to their current emotional state, but by conveying encouragement through the statement "I would love to learn more about the events that led to your feelings," you are establishing yourself as a safe space of connection. This may have the benefit of interrupting subconscious patterns of distrust to show them how different this moment can be, no matter how difficult life was before. Whether through this supportive sentence or any question your heart longs to ask, you begin to discover the unending fulfillment of true intimacy that emerges from stepping out of your comfort zone and daring to reach out.

Encouragement in Action

By learning how to hold space and offering an encouraging, thoughtful presence, you are sure to further your own healing journey.

Perhaps you find yourself unexpectedly becoming the softest, most comforting shoulder for a coworker to cry on after they've received shocking news about a close relative. No matter how uncomfortable or unexpected it may seem, you can hold them in your arms or even in your thoughts, allowing them to feel greater support in whatever way you're inspired to give it.

Maybe you're holding the hand of a dying relative, healing wounds of neglect by offering the kindness they didn't have the capacity to provide you. Instead of sitting in anticipation of an apology you've waited to hear most of your life, the attribute of encouragement inspires you to lead by loving example. From this space, you will be uplifted by the depth of your contribution, no longer hoping to receive from those who may have nothing left to give.

Instead of responding critically to hateful comments on social media posts, you can use your supportive statement of encouragement to open the doorway of safety. Since people worldwide converge on comment threads, your most encouraging responses will help others learn more supportive ways to engage with one another.

Rather than creating more division by condemning those who judge, place you in categories of generalization, or are hungry to debate about political parties or hidden agendas, the attribute of encouragement simply invites you to acknowledge the activities of another person's despair. If you react to their unconsciousness from *your* most unhealed parts, you will give their wounds the power to overwhelm and exhaust you. Conversely, by being aware of their pain, you will be responding to the consciousness within them, no matter how deeply buried it seems to be. Imagine answering someone who has lashed out at you with "I see that you're in pain." Perhaps the acknowledgment of their inner conflict helps further their evolution and deepens bonds of intimacy instead of creating more discord.

If you're confronted by someone of a different race, gender, or belief system who demands to know your active role in the healing of social injustice, how will the attribute of encouragement inspire you to respond? Since you can't know a person's point of view unless you've walked lifetimes in their shoes, perhaps you can invite someone affected by atrocity, gender disparity, marginalization, or racial profiling to share their most gripping experiences. By saying, "I would love to hear more about the events that led to your feelings," you ask to understand their despair more deeply, ensuring that you will continue to be a greater living solution to their plight.

What if it's not a matter of apologizing for the brutality you didn't perpetrate personally but of giving others a more conscious, loving example of the gender or race that wounded them with bigotry and persecution? Through the attribute of encouragement, you come to understand the concept of privilege as the honor of helping to resolve the continual mistreatment of those who walk among and came before you.

This is the power of embodied love. It is the very compassion and patience required to transform this planet through a depth of healing that holding space provides. It's why, regardless of each scenario or circumstance, being helpful always begins with listening.

Encouragement as a Daily Practice

To bring the attribute of encouragement to the forefront of your awareness, try one or all of these daily practices:

- To learn how to listen beyond the surface level of agreement, turn on the news, and despite the narrative of each story or the opinions presented, mindfully use each report as a deliberate practice to encourage the livelihood of the people on the screen. If a news anchor is speaking, dare to focus on how wonderful it is that they're living their dream, rather than judging the words they're scripted to say.

  If stories involving misfortune are presented, instead of turning away from intensity, dare to use them as an opportunity to hold space. If any segment becomes painful to watch, see if you can simply take a few breaths to remind your body that it's able to relax and remain open in the safety of your presence.

- To deepen the selfless quality of encouragement, the next time you meet someone for lunch or speak on the phone, allow your primary objective to be encouraging their journey by asking engaging questions about their life. As you lead with authentic heartfelt interest, only share the details of your own life when others ask specific questions. This may initially trigger your core wounds that no one ever sees or hears you. Yet, those who have the space and capacity to receive you always do so by asking questions of interest. Imagine deliberately entering a conversation with the intention to support another, knowing that you'll discover a more miraculous form of fulfillment when you're excited to encourage them without being attached to how much they offer you in return.

- As a helpful habit to cultivate the attribute of encouragement, go through the contact list on your cell phone and send someone you know an encouraging text message, just to remind them that they're seen and supported in life.

CHAPTER 2

It's Not a Matter of What Anyone Else *Doesn't* Know

My parents reflected so many important life lessons, sometimes not through the wisdom they shared but through the confusing ways they would behave. For instance, they tended to express the strength of their own intelligence by criticizing people around them. Whether they were decompressing from stressful workdays or hanging out with neighbors, they seemed to show little empathy toward the struggles others might be facing. Their interactions seemed to me like an ongoing comedy roast of other people's pain as a way to blow off the steam they only knew how to bottle up.

I found solace playing video games in my bedroom, so I could block out their chorus of mean-spirited cackling. Yet, I felt so much pain from the cruelty they projected onto others. The volume of my parents' embellishments would amplify in the presence of a live, receptive audience. When they were among friends who perceived others just as judgmentally as they did, this kind of behavior created a sense of normalcy among them.

Instinctively, I knew this was not the way I wanted to grow up.

It's one thing to experience bullying in school from kids who suppress their insecurities by overpowering others, but it was an entirely different dynamic to see such destructive behavior surface in the two people I trusted the most and whose love I yearned for. Their denigrations of others always felt like a personal betrayal, even when I wasn't the target of their verbal attacks. Because I could feel in my body how they gossiped about others, I often responded privately with tears streaming down my cheeks—as if I were the subject of their criticism.

I confronted my parents one morning after a particularly disturbing gossip party. "That was loud last night," I said.

"I'm sorry, honey," my mom replied. "We were just having a good time."

This confused me, so I pressed on, "You had fun, but said mean things."

My parents, both acting as if they had no idea what I was referring to, asked me, "Who said mean things, Matthew?"

Although I feared I might become the next object of their disapproval, I replied, "You did. About others. Your boss. The server at the restaurant . . ."

They could see how much this bothered me. With both of them now rooted in good-parent mode, they responded, "We were kidding. That's just what adults do."

After they both hugged me, I returned to the safe haven of my room, now even more perplexed about why such hurtful actions seemed so normal to them.

As I grew, I would further process these painful memories to help me understand the patterning I'd witnessed. I soon recognized the wounds both of my parents carried. My mom carried wounds of disappointment and abandonment from her pathologically lying father. When she became his power of attorney after he had a stroke, his dishonesty and incompetence ramped up, and she quickly grew intolerant of his deceptive behavior. Whenever she witnessed what she perceived as incompetence in others, she would unknowingly unleash on them all the fury she couldn't express to the man whose lifelong mental complications left her feeling abandoned, invisible, and disempowered.

My father carried the wound of judgment from both of his parents. Born in an era when dyslexia had not yet been established as a diagnosable condition and was viewed instead as a sign of stupidity, my dad defied the desires of both of his parents by forging his own life direction. Instead of going to medical school, becoming a surgeon, and taking over his father's private medical practice, he spit in the face of their expectations and vowed to achieve success on his own terms as a salesman.

Both of my parents became successful in their respective fields and proudly raised my sister and me in bustling suburban America. But all too often, my mom would be quick to project her view of incompetence onto others, while my dad cast the label of "stupid" as freely as it was once projected onto him. From an adult standpoint, I began to see how both would use the distractions of other people to avoid the pain and disappointment they thought had given their parents some sort of power over them.

I remember as a kid asking my mom how she felt about her father. "Don't even get me started," she'd reply.

"You seem upset," I said.

This stopped her in her tracks. She leaned in toward me with the most intense glare and said, "I won't even give that man the satisfaction of affecting me."

My dad entered the scene and politely guided me toward my bedroom saying, "Your mom had a rough day."

As I retreated to my room and closed the door, my mom began projecting her emotional pain onto my dad. "Why are you asking me so many questions after what I've gone through?" she demanded.

This made him feel inadequate, so he fired back, "I'm just trying to understand. Why are you attacking me?"

Even though my parents' arguments literally felt like the two sides of my brain battling with each other, their conflicts became strangely fascinating to me. They each held against their spouse what they believed the other person didn't know. As my mom and dad went twelve rounds of verbal sparring, trying to convince the other of how wrong he or she was, the volume and intensity continued to escalate. I was afraid they might hurt each other, a neighbor might hear the fight and call the police, or they might even threaten divorce.

I knew deep down that my parents' love couldn't survive without their codependency on one another. From an early age, I took it upon myself to be their ongoing crisis counselor. It was a desperate attempt to squash their conflict in the hope that I would find some relief from our family dynamic. While my involvement would become another facet of codependency infiltrating the household, I just couldn't help myself when their arguments reached a certain boiling point. I would burst out of my room, yelling at both of them to quiet down before the police showed up. Then I would turn to my mom and explain, "He is just trying to love you!"

She would immediately play the victim with, "Why are you attacking me?"

Then my dad would enter the fray: "Don't talk to your mother that way!"

His words brought the deep sting of betrayal. *Mom's inner monster is beating you to a pulp*, I would think, *and now you're going to come to her defense to help lessen the damage when you both step into your bedroom for further arguing?* I was incensed.

While I initially used my pattern of rescuing others to cope with the sudden outbursts of emotional volatility around me, it would take on a more subtle context as I began working as an empathic healer. In the first few years of my healing career, I developed the perfect recipe for further codependency: I defined myself as a spiritual rescuer who surrounded himself with those who yearned to be rescued. I offered insights to audiences, but somehow I couldn't shake the feeling that I wasn't truly helping them learn how to hold space for themselves. The more I witnessed my tendency to rescue or even interrupt someone's sharing with an intuition "I just had to bring through," the more I began seeing the limitations of this approach.

The deeper solution that helped me buffer my inner spiritual rescuer came when I surfaced memories of my parents' judgmental tendencies. In revisiting these moments from a more objective perspective, my intuition would ask me, *What adjective best describes your parents' behavior?* The answer that came was *invalidating*. My intuition would then ask, *What is the opposite of invalidation?* Immediately I knew, the answer was *validation*.

In receiving this insight, I began challenging myself to be a space of validation for other people's experiences. As the attribute of validation began maturing within me, I recognized new horizons of healing potential. It was no longer a matter of what anyone didn't know or needed to figure out, but rather the space I could so lovingly hold to allow their deepest truths to be realized. This was the moment I felt I was being of true healing service, no matter how much rescuing anyone wanted from me.

The Attribute of Validation

As the second attribute in holding space, validation offers the gift of acceptance of someone's personal struggle. While it can be easy to imagine how much better off someone might be if only they knew what you see so clearly from your vantage point, the deepest insights most often arise as a result of the validation you offer instead of the course corrections you might impose. Whether with the best of intentions or from an agenda of trying to make someone more like who you want them to be, any pattern of rescuing often leads to misunderstandings. This is especially true when rushing others toward the greater perspectives they may not be ready to receive, process, and accept.

Admittedly, it can be difficult to surrender the tendency to rescue since the alternative feels like watching people suffer. When you're unable to stop the pain or resolve the confusion that someone experiences, it can elicit deep guilt in you—as if you're furthering their agony if you can't help them shift. But, just as a butterfly won't survive the cocooning process without mustering the strength to break free on its own, the people in your life can't wholeheartedly internalize the inevitability of positive change unless they've arrived at their own internal conclusions.

No matter how intensely you want others to change or how much better life could be if only they would see things differently, true compassion allows healing to take place at its own pace. Once someone's pain has been validated, a greater space can open up and emerge for further transformation to unfold. This may not occur at the moment you want it to, but rather, as an expression of divine timing that knows the precise depth of experience everyone needs in order to expand from one level of consciousness to the next.

When you validate someone, you help them see their subjective reality as purposeful and valuable for the unique journey they are on. Whether it's an expression of their highest truth suddenly dawning on them or just a tiny step forward in a series of evolutionary moves, these perspectives don't have to be the highest truth in order for them to act as stepping stones toward a greater awareness. When someone is validated, they can sense a moment of connection that helps them remember they're not alone, although it may feel to them as if they're the only one in the world enduring such hardship. Even when the way someone views a moment seems so out of sync with the most obvious reality, you are more likely to help them awaken into greater perspectives through the loving support of validation than any impulse toward rescuing. This doesn't mean that you agree to see a moment exactly as someone else does. Rather, you are supporting their growth by confirming the experience they're having.

For example, if someone says to you, "I am having a bad day," a person expressing the attribute of validation would reply, "I really understand the bad day you're having." You are not agreeing with how this person distinguishes bad days from good ones but affirming their experience as a universal circumstance that each of us faces.

Conversely, if someone says, "I am having a bad day," your inner rescuer might say, "Here's what I would do if I were you," or "I hate to say I told you so." If your inner rescuer has adopted a spiritual persona, you may think you are helping them by looking for a wide array of superstitiously fueled spiritual problems. In order to save them from the depths of their most profound healing journey you might suggest the following:

- "Maybe your vibration is too low."

- "You should just go manifest something different."

- "What did you do horribly wrong in a past life?"

- "Maybe you're in resistance."

- "I think your chakras are tangled up."

- "What sign are you?"

- "What number are you on the enneagram chart?"

- "You must not be vegan."

- "You have entities, don't you!"

These are just a few examples of how the ego uses spiritual concepts to blame a person for the experience they're having. This is a form of victim shaming. While a rescuer may insist on having the best intentions, the impulse to save people leaves those people in pain feeling defeated, unseen, and invalidated during moments when the presence of companionship is the only helpful gift they need.

Even when the other person begs to be rescued, you are much better off holding space for the healing already underway than helping them avoid their process.

Through the attribute of validation, you agree to support people no matter how they view each moment. Because the subconscious mind often categorizes information by similarities and differences, a person's ego cannot affirm the truth of your perspective without equally feeling that they are wrong in their own. While someone might agree with you, they're likely to walk away feeling defeated—another instance in which they gave away their power. Perhaps from this vantage point, you can see how, in order to help someone truly heal, it's far more useful to demonstrate support rather than offering corrections.

While we each navigate our own journey and face a multitude of emotional experiences, they often occur in a different order from one person to the next. Throughout each lifetime, all of the insights you have and will receive are realizations that everyone else is bound to explore. But perhaps they are shuffled in a specific order or sequence to serve the uniqueness of their journey that may differ from how your path unfolds.

Through the attribute of validation, you bring a sense of acceptance to the experiences people often judge as punishments, especially when situations develop in undesirable ways. When validation replaces the unconscious tendency to rescue, you are able to help others remember that their experiences haven't occurred by chance or mistake. There is a reason each person faces all they do, and it's not a result of their wrongdoing. While no amount of convincing can instill this wisdom in another person, once validated for the experience they're already having, they can open to unexpected change with renewed faith, greater courage, and a deeper sense of interconnection.

For example, let's say you are spending time with a friend who is at their wit's end. They may say, "I just don't know what to do!" While your inner rescuer already has five suggestions ready to launch, along with graphs, pie charts, and a PowerPoint presentation to prove your case, your inner space holder knows it's not a matter of what anyone doesn't know. While it can be easy to assume it's your role to shift someone's experience for the better, your inner space holder offers the gift of companionship that helps others realize how okay they are—no matter how confused, displaced, or out of sorts they may feel.

In addition, in order to embrace the true power of validation, it's important to distinguish how validating someone's experience differs from placating them. Placating is an unconscious act of blindly agreeing with someone else's beliefs, viewpoints, and perceptions. When placating, one might nod in approval and say, "I agree with you," "Yeah, totally!" "For sure!" instead of, "Thank you for sharing this. You have a right to be heard." While coming from a rather innocent place, we often placate to appease someone else, mainly as a way to keep the peace and avoid rejection. While it's natural to want to sidestep the pain of mistreatment and maximize the pleasure of interpersonal connection, holding space can only occur once we no longer hide behind facades of blind agreement.

In the absence of placating or rescuing, the attribute of validation helps others find greater acceptance within the framework of their own circumstances without spoiling any "aha" moments that life will send their way.

Even when holding space for yourself, the inclination to either placate or correct your mind only furthers the imbalances you may feel. While it's common to crave a new life direction when you're the most stuck, it's actually the grace of supportive companionship with yourself that allows the sense of urgency or being in survival mode to dissipate. When holding space for yourself, it's not a matter of what you or anyone else needs to know. Instead, it is your ability to find greater resilience in the aftermath of defeat, clarity at the height of confusion, and renewed strength in the depth of despair by how lovingly you embrace and value your own needs.

Through the attribute of validation, you're able to feel a greater depth of support that helps you remain open to the evolutionary value of human experiences, whether during periods of external displacement, inner transition, or feeling light-years away from the highlight reel you had hoped your life would be.

What Could Possibly Go Wrong?

Through the space-holding process, you may encounter people who ask for support but only want you to help them by agreeing with their viewpoint. Since this isn't the purpose of validation, there is no reason to take to heart how someone reacts when living in a reality they can't control to their liking. Here are some common judgments that others can project onto you when you choose to validate their experience instead of agreeing with their opinion:

- Some individuals may claim you're being unsupportive if you haven't blindly agreed with how they handled a situation.

- There are those who will shame themselves and blame you for shaming them when you're merely giving them the right to be—while peacefully having your own unique responses to life.

- Some people may be so geared toward bypassing the intensity of their feelings or responsibility for their behavior that they place all their power in your hands as their most preferred rescuer.

- It's possible that the depth of someone's sharing runs out the clock on your schedule of commitments. If you're unable to stay with them for as long as they had hoped, they may label you another abandoner in their lives despite all the time, work, and energy you've devoted to hearing them with attentive presence.

- You may have even indulged the invitation to rescue on numerous occasions, only to realize that your efforts never amount to long-lasting change.

Others may put you in these predicaments or perhaps you are playing these patterns out with them. All the while, you will know in the depths of your heart that your presence in someone's life doesn't offer greater benefit if you blindly agree or adopt their enemies as your own. It's also true that holding an objective space so that someone's feelings can pour out doesn't make you aloof, noncommittal, or avoidant.

When you choose to hold space, you are blessed with a tangible opportunity to support the needs of others, even when all they can do is resist and writhe in despair. Just like your post-surgical pain wouldn't stop those who love you from visiting you in the hospital, you are equally able to be a steadfast validator of each human experience, even when it seems as if whatever you say or do doesn't makes a bit of difference. Remember, you aren't supporting others as a way to control the outcome of their experiences. You are validating the feelings they share, even when they're conveyed from a perspective that differs from your own.

Some people are so embroiled in hating their own experiences that they may view you as a problem if you don't have the solutions they demand. However, while you may not be in a position to give them exactly what they want, you are always capable of offering companionship and support as a heart-centered witness and validator of human evolution.

Setting an Intention for Validation

To release the pattern of rescuing and hold a space of validation for yourself and others, please repeat the following words out loud:

I intend to hold space through the attribute of validation for myself and others without playing the role of a rescuer. I allow validation to be offered from a space of faithfulness and love, as an offering of companionship for the resolution of all. I recognize that all the wise insights within me are the same ones growing in the hearts of every person, perhaps dawning in their awareness in different ways and at different times than they have blossomed in me. In knowing the gift of immaculate support is how I can assist myself and those I love during moments of pain and uncertainty, I release all judgments, as well as each tendency to need rescuing or to rescue others, no matter how deeply my ego insists on what anyone needs to know.

I allow the validation I offer to support the openness of all, no matter how it's received, overlooked, or denied, or whether I agree with the viewpoints of any personal sharing. If and when this hurts my feelings, triggers memories of past traumas, makes me more distrusting of others, or causes me to shut down in rejection or lash out in resentment, I allow myself the sacred space to be with my feelings and offer the gift of validation to any invalidated part of me. I honor the gift of validation as a way of reminding others of the support that's always around them, even when all hope seems lost, or they are at the brink of despair. Whether given to me, another person, or as active blessings to humanity, I welcome and allow the attribute of validation to show me a renewed depth of faithfulness, commitment, and dedication that comes from the grace of being open, no matter how shut down or disempowered others may be. And so it is.

The Supportive Statement of Validation

"You Have a Right to Be Heard"

Validation is a depth of support that invites everyone's innocence to come out of hiding. Whether life's most daunting traumas have suppressed the power of your voice or even silenced it, the attribute of validation helps each damaged part know, despite the past, that it is now safe to step forward and let a testimony of survival be acknowledged. This is why the most supportive statement the attribute of validation can offer is "You have a right to be heard."

While every living being has survived moments of unthinkable hardship, the fundamental level of emotional processing occurs through the power of one's voice. This processing may begin with a person attempting to rationalize sequences of past events, trying to make greater sense of the inconceivable nature of mean-spiritedness, vindictive reactions, selfish tendencies, and unconscionable behavior. The more often each person is invited to sound their experience, the deeper the sharing can go. This is why healing and intimate connection are rooted in the sharing of feelings and are never a matter of what anyone does or doesn't know.

In truth, you may feel uncomfortable sharing how deeply other people's actions have affected you. You may feel apprehensive when others share their pain, since it evokes in you memories of how you may have treated another innocent being or how others have treated you. You may dislike how slowly the voice opens up to heal, despite how quickly the mind insists on rushing through the events that still linger in memory. As you may come to recognize, perhaps now more than ever, the ability to heal doesn't always unfold at the speed of personal desire.

For all that you or anyone in life has endured, a true depth of healing deserves a gentle pace—so that you can clearly see how each piece of a shattered heart is put back together with miraculous precision. This is why "You have a right to be heard" is such a powerful gift of validation that has nothing to do with whether you agree with someone's standpoint or how passionately they may disagree with you.

If you overlook the importance of allowing others to be heard and lead with rescuing, your attempts to fast-track their process keeps them just as silenced as when their wounds were created. Imagine trying to have the final word in a conversation in which you are hoping to "talk sense" into someone, only to stop mid-sentence and realize that you are helping perpetuate the silence of victimhood by speaking when this might be the other person's golden opportunity to share.

When you're unattached to if and how sharing occurs, you are merely using the power of space holding to remind others of their inherent right and freedom to express the voice they have been given. In contrast to the controlling mechanism of rescuing, you are not here to dictate the terms and conditions of healing, no matter how much relief you "know" the person may feel once they're ready to open up. Rather, through the laws of unity consciousness, the role you play in supporting someone's right to speak helps you to reclaim the power of your own voice that past events may have silenced.

However, while the attribute of validation reminds us that everyone has a right to be heard, you may feel uncomfortable hearing the words others need to say. They might even paint you as a character in their lives that differs from how you want to be seen. It may trigger impatience and the tendency to defend yourself against someone's viewpoints when their primal expression of sharing breaks every conceptual law in the spiritual playbook. It may involve the repeating of content they've already gone over or tendencies to loop in blame, questions of negotiation, or a constant desire for others' approval. If you have it in your heart to offer someone the grace of your most thoughtful attentive presence, then let it also be their gift to open, receive, avoid, or deny in any way they choose.

Validation in Action

The attribute of validation leads with empowering others to openly share as opposed to leading with the conceptual advice a rescuer desperately needs to convey.

Perhaps you are the first person a loved one calls after receiving disappointing news at a custody hearing. What if blame, harshness, and accusation are exactly what they need to express, not because it's the deepest truth, but because it represents layers of protection they must voice before more vulnerable feelings can surface?

Maybe you are the safest space for someone to report abuse to, despite how intensely the fear of retribution has paralyzed them. What if sitting with them and holding their hand with gentle comfort as their thoughts come out in sentences, fragments, or word by word is exactly what they need to feel true safety?

Even when interacting with others on social media posts, responding to someone else's blame with the words "You have a right to be heard" helps invite their innocence to go deeper into their own emotional experience, whether or not they are willing to "go there."

What if allowing someone you know to be heard by expressing their most hurtful sharing helps release just enough pent up emotion to spare a couple or family from the destructive cycle of domestic violence?

What if simply by suggesting "You have a right to be heard," you are helping to support someone on the brink of collapse through a journey of emotional redemption?

Perhaps you unexpectedly bear witness to a friend's relapse in addiction. Maybe just by sitting with them during dark moments of regret, you might help them recommit to a recovery process instead of burying their lack of self-worth under layers of judgment and more intense self-harm.

While you can't be responsible for anyone's actions other than your own, through the awareness of holding space, you begin to recognize moments when you deepen your own self-acceptance by the validating role you play in someone else's life. This can occur even while being true to the limited amount of time you have to give, which might disappoint those who can only see life through the eyes of pain and lack. No matter the differences in experience, you can rest in knowing the positive impact you're having just by reminding others that they are never alone and are always being supported, no matter how things seem to be.

Validation as a Daily Practice

To bring the attribute of validation to the forefront of your awareness, try one or all of these daily practices:

- Aspire to view the discomfort of your experience or the circumstances of others like a meditation. Each time the tendency to rescue arises, simply take a moment to breathe, listen on a deeper level, and validate the uniqueness of the other person's reality.

- Notice how your experience with hurtful feelings and even pain transforms when you validate how you feel, including how much you dislike feeling this way.

- The next time you feel compelled to share a rant on social media, turn it into an uncensored journal entry for only your eyes to read. Dare to see the difference between searching for outside agreement online versus validating yourself through the intimacy of journal writing.

CHAPTER 3

You Can't Rush What Has Been Buried for So Long

While most of my childhood friends ignored the difficulties of their family dynamics, the discord in my home was so intense, it felt as if it were taking place within my own body. While everyone is destined to be empathic, my capacity for openness was such that I never knew turning away was a viable option. I even recall wishing I could be sick or need to go to the hospital, since any time I was ill, my parents' most loving qualities emerged. I cried myself to sleep many nights because of how difficult the intensity of my family dynamics felt. It wasn't as if my parents were always personifying their least redeemable qualities. Yet, when push came to shove, I felt as if I was being raised by two hard-working, emotional hand grenades.

I remember one particular night around the age of eleven when I was crying out to be rescued. I begged God to come get me.

"Please take me back. I don't want to be here," I pleaded. I was hoping that just like in the movies, the moment someone asks for help, the hero enters to save the day. But no one came. Just the sound of my deepest sorrow pouring out of my face and into my pillow.

On that night, my tears hit a crescendo—then suddenly they stopped. Out of nowhere, I no longer felt the deep reservoir of loneliness and despair but rather a visceral sense of my own presence supporting me from within. Instead of wondering when someone would come to save me, I was soothed, acknowledged, and supported by—myself. It was as if there were two parts of me: an innocent empathic kid trying to make sense of life in a physical body and a column of light that existed within this childlike persona holding me in a way I had always yearned to be held.

From a lifelong fascination with superheroes, the space I now held for myself felt as if a larger-than-life, bionic character had rescued me. It wasn't as if I never cried again. I just didn't feel as isolated from others when the tears came. This significant moment of space holding also inspired moments of appreciation for the emotions I was willing to feel so openly. Rather than looking to others for approval, I began to honor myself for the courage it took to be so vulnerable. This created an intriguing road map of memories in which each instance of deep emotional pain also contained the soothing awareness that my inner superhero would show up, carry me through, and acknowledge my openness as a strength instead of a weakness.

Throughout my journey, no matter how insurmountable the obstacles felt, it never occurred to me to search for an exit strategy. I knew intuitively that each layer would heal. Because of the support I felt from within, I had no instinct to chase away my wounds or imagine anything was missing in my life by having to face them. This was how I began to realize over a span of many years, you can't rush what has been buried for so long.

The Attribute of Reverence

Through the attribute of reverence, you honor each person's will and determination to face the intensity of their pain. Rather than understanding someone's discomfort as a circumstance they must be rescued from, you gain a deeper awareness in noticing incredible transitions from one level of consciousness to the next whenever their growing pains begin to surface.

Through the attribute of reverence, you may realize one profound truth: *No one actually needs different circumstances, they only need greater support for the experiences they're having.* Life often gets so out of balance that unless you are rescuing yourself or others from difficulty, it's easy to imagine you must be a contributor to the suffering all around you. Just as when children feel the growing pains that mark the transition from childhood to adolescence, there is nothing you can do to interrupt the process but to decide how much love you are capable of giving.

The beauty of reverence allows you to have a more compassionate view of hardship. From this vantage point, everything is bound to change, including your most negative perceptions of daunting circumstances. While it's a true measure of grace to be grounded and heart-centered through the healing process, it is equally acceptable to feel angry, hurt, lonely, and even confused, since the pain of difficult events is always a part of the greater transformation taking place.

Even when you're unable to be physically present with someone during life's most dire moments, the attribute of reverence offers potent healing that you can always share from a distance. Just by imagining how a person's current circumstances are helping them grow into higher qualities, your perspective sends them greater support through the power of unity consciousness. This can help them see redeemable benefits that often masquerade as nuisance, annoyance, frustration, and difficulty.

This is why the attribute of reverence is the remedy for rescuing. It differs greatly from the old paradigm of healing in which you may fear that someone will be stuck in the depths of excruciating pain until they can somehow shift into a higher awareness. That would be like telling a child, "Your growing pains will stop once you see this more like an adult." Since you can't rush what has been buried for so long, informing someone during their most debilitating moments that relief is solely dependent on their capabilities will only distract from their healing. While it would seem outlandishly unfair to top off someone's most painful ordeal with that type of unhelpful pressure, many people tend to embrace this belief. They insist that their evolution is a race against time, where they will make more room for pleasure and less for pain as soon as they figure out a way to "get it all right."

Whether you offer your gifts of reverence up close or from afar, you are providing incredible doses of emotional support without needing the other person to change and even without knowing the exact benefit you're providing.

In the depths of your own turmoil, you can always call upon the Universe to be your grand space holder so that you don't overwhelm yourself in attempting to fast-track your own healing. If you wouldn't push someone else to change their viewpoint during waves of pain or panic, then the same applies when holding space for yourself. You can always say inwardly, *I know these difficult experiences are bringing out more of my best, even if I can't sense it now.* If you're asking the Universe for greater support during your loneliest moments of growth, you can always inwardly declare, *Thank you beloved Universe for working through me and providing the perspectives of reverence and greater support I desire.*

Even if you're unable to be in the same location as another person, you can always offer reverence by saying to yourself, *Dear beloved Universe, thank you for sending the gift of reverence to _____ for the greater good of their journey. And so it is.*

Through the attribute of reverence, you feel less helpless in life by learning how to share from a space of helpfulness. When you're able to sense the beauty of expansion growing in yourself and others, you exist on the same side as Universal Will. This is the realm of divine timing: the energy of miracles, synchronicity, and alchemical magic. While it certainly isn't a power anyone can control, the more aligned with reverence you are, the greater the possibility that divine timing will enter your awareness. This is why each of us is blessed to coexist in the presence of others. For even in moments of debilitation, the empathy connecting all hearts will pray for the healing of others to bring the miracles those who suffer may be unable to access on their own.

I've seen on many occasions how someone whose healing journey has brought them to a place of overwhelming pain inspires friends and family to come together as one. Responses such as candlelight vigils, prayer circles, crowdfunding campaigns, and viral social media posts assist in the healing of a loved one, while their need for healing helps activate a renewed level of compassion in the friends, family, and sometimes even strangers called upon to participate. It's why, through the space-holding process, every moment of authentic giving is also an unexpected blessing to be received.

While it may seem impossible to erase another person's despair or help them see their life from a new perspective, the key to reverence is recognizing that you always have a choice in how you view any moment. Through the eyes of reverence, you can send waves of support to someone in need just by recognizing the strength and conviction they are cultivating by enduring the healing taking place.

There are fear-based spiritual myths that suggest that the more you turn toward adverse experiences, even in a positive way, the longer they're likely to stay. Yet, how could this be true, when denying, bypassing, or ignoring difficulties does nothing to make them budge. If fighting your experiences with a fury of judgment and denial hasn't helped set you free, how is befriending them with kindness and respect making them stay? Ultimately, you may see this myth as totally irrational. Yet, it can still hold a power over you, especially if you have no other focus than wanting adversity to stop.

From your new space-holding perspective, the more often you are inspired by helpfulness, the less helpless you will feel. As you become more supportive and engaging during the moments of healing that no one can control, you are able to develop a greater capacity of presence and embody it more consistently.

What Could Possibly Go Wrong?

From the dynamic listening of encouragement to the compassion offered through validation, we now turn a more assertive corner to reverence. Of course, not everyone will resonate with the affirming support you give them for how incredibly strong they must be to have lived through their ordeal. This is especially true when their conditioning suggests they shut down in emotional protest until the experience they oppose ends. Because the attribute of reverence invites you to make the most of any situation, it's common for those in pain to project their resentment at having to face onslaughts of discomfort, difficulty, and inconvenience.

This is why it's essential to always hold space for yourself. In this way, you will develop the courage to share openly, while not taking so personally the battles others have with outcomes they can't control. While you certainly don't want to be someone else's target, the deeper you go into the beauty of space holding, the more those you are blessed to support during difficult times will inspire your most heartfelt responses. Step-by-step, moment by moment, and offering by offering, you increase the likelihood that life will bring out your best to support the best in others—and without you always needing a crisis for your greatest offerings to emerge.

While you're cultivating such benefits, the question remains, What could possibly go wrong? Since it has been said that "misery loves company," it's possible that someone won't appreciate your support, especially if it means being more open, accepting, and receptive during moments they only wish to escape. This is why the attribute of reverence can always be your silent gift of embodied presence, particularly when hostile waters become too choppy. You certainly don't have to convince anyone that what you see is true. Perhaps you might just offer a loving smile, even if it's a gift the other person is unable to take in. Since reverence only provides the gift of companionship, others may become emotionally triggered if they perceive you as yet one more person who has no ability to diminish the intensity of their circumstances.

Certainly, when you're in a parenting role, it can be a daunting, heartbreaking task to support the emotional well-being of children who lash out when they're in the midst of difficult experiences. Even when they judge you as less capable than the idealized parent they wish they had, on a higher level, you can acknowledge their lashing out as a trauma response to unexpected change or long-lasting pain. If you remember your own childhood, most likely you went through moments of growth you may have believed you wouldn't survive. Yet, somehow you did. Life even escorted you into exciting new chapters along your evolutionary path, which is exactly the process others are in, whether they know it or not.

Sometimes you'll be so fulfilled and uplifted by your ability to give from a space of reverence, you will feel totally immune to other people's behavior. In other instances, the reactions of another may instigate a breaking point of emotional release that will require you to find greater safety to hold space for yourself. Through no fault of your own, your personal crisis might even bring people into deeper empathic despair, as they lead more with fear than the faith you hope to feel from them.

In moments of uncertainty, no matter how someone interprets your most thoughtful intentions, you are always planting seeds in the quantum field. Through the offering of reverence, you are filling up each person's energy field like an emotional bank account with the blessings they will receive at exactly the moment their heart is ready to open.

Setting an Intention for Reverence

To release the pattern of righteousness and hold a space of reverence for yourself and others, please repeat the following words out loud:

I intend to hold space through the attribute of reverence for myself and others without filtering it through righteous beliefs or controlling behavior. I allow reverence to be provided from a space of openness and grace, as a gift of complimentary perspective for the well-being of all. I recognize how I may attempt to change someone's experience, including my own, as a trauma response throughout the healing process. I accept that this response comes from a feeling of helplessness, which heals as I choose to be helpful, no matter how big or small a contribution I make. In knowing the gift of heart-centered companionship is how I can assist myself and those I love during moments of despair, I release all tendencies of righteousness, no matter how well-intended my ego insists them to be.

From this space, I allow the attribute of reverence to support the relief and freedom of all, no matter how it is received, overlooked, or denied, or whether I agree with the viewpoints of any personal sharing. If and when this hurts my feelings, triggers memories of past traumas, makes me more distrusting of others, or causes me to shut down in rejection or lash out in resentment, I allow myself the sacred space to be with my feelings and offer the gift of reverence to any part of me. I honor the attribute of reverence as a way of reminding others of the strengths and connections around them, no matter how displaced or disconnected anyone seems to be. Whether given to myself or another person or as an active blessing to humanity, I welcome and allow the attribute of reverence to show me a renewed depth of presence that can meet others in crisis without taking it on as my own issue to process. And so it is.

The Supportive Statement of Reverence

"I Am Here with You"

Sometimes the greatest moments of misunderstanding occur when you don't know what to say in response to someone's dilemma. While you might feel the impulse to rescue that can come across as more righteous than helpful, the thoughtfulness you embody always brings the greatest benefit. That's why the most supportive sentence that reverence provides is simply "I am here with you."

Even if you're unable to be in someone's physical presence, you can say "I am here with you" as a prayer sent through the ether or as encouraging words spoken on the phone. In this way, you meet that person's perception of helplessness with helpful offerings of support. While many people fear being a burden in the lives of others, the statement "I am here with you," can help ease tension when they show up as their least capable selves.

Whatever response your statement of reverence inspires—from sarcastic eye rolls to tears of heartfelt relief—you formulate long-lasting bonds of allegiance with the Universe through your willingness to support others. When "I am here with you" replaces "I am here to save you" or the self-righteousness of "Here's what I would do if I were you," you help others discover the worthiness of being seen and heard, no matter how often they yearn to run and hide.

When you're holding space for the tensions and releases orbiting your own reality, you can gently soften your resentment when others are not showing up for you by reminding yourself that you are always here as your own greatest supporter. If this feels like a disappointing consolation prize, it is most likely due to playing the role of a character who has waited for others to provide the constant unwavering support that always dwells within. The more you spend meaningful time holding space for your own experience, the more attentive you will be in fulfilling your needs. Even if you are at your wit's end and are unsure of how much more you can endure, you can always call upon the Universe for greater support.

From this space, you can realize that the most insurmountable odds will create an equally fertile ground of evolving expansion and connection for those who dare to lean in with interest, even when everything seems to be falling apart.

Reverence in Action

Through the attribute of reverence, you will recognize the true value of others by bringing greater attention to the strength, character, and determination it takes for them to endure and survive each moment.

What if a pregnant friend's water breaks early, and you are the only one to support them through unexpected childbirth? While the adrenaline surging through your body may yearn to help the baby be delivered as quickly as possible, through the gift of reverence, you are there to be fully present for the experience you are helping your friend through. It may be a quick delivery or a more drawn-out process. Either way, you have been placed along your friend's path to so compassionately remind them, "I am here with you."

Maybe you are undergoing treatment for an illness and find yourself far too exhausted to hold space for yourself. This is the perfect opportunity to ask the Universe to work through you and provide such gifts on your behalf.

Perhaps you are estranged from your family, children, or a loved one, either by your choice or theirs. Whenever the pain of this conflict orbits your awareness, take a moment to visualize them happy, radiant, healthy, and free—as blessings for everyone involved.

What if you are near someone who shrinks in your presence or perceives you as a threat based on gender, race, or any other outward form of appearance? What if simply offering a smile or a supportive statement, such as "We're all in this together," helps ease their history of tension?

When you're online, your supportive statement, "I am here with you," goes a long way to offer compassion to others, even if their only conceivable solution is finding an escape from pain. Through the reverence you offer, you join the Universe in supporting life's most harrowing stages of transformation that often don't come wrapped in the prettiest packaging.

Out of profound respect for the trajectory each person is on, when you lead with reverence, the intensity of helplessness transforms into moments of inspiration, especially if you remember that *no one actually needs different circumstances, they only need greater support for the experiences they are having.*

Reverence as a Daily Practice

To bring the attribute of reverence to the forefront of your awareness, try one or all of these daily practices:

- Think of someone from your past whose memory brings up a sense of you holding a personal grudge. Write the name of the person who hurt you in the first blank space below. In the next space, write an adjective that best describes how your experience with them made you feel. In the third space, write its opposite. Whether as a spoken declaration or a written exercise, you can process deeper pain through the attribute of reverence by accepting this statement: "No matter how much _____ made me feel _____, it has inspired a deeper

healing to bring me into greater union with _____
even when I have yet to see such results in my life."

- Whether in response to a horrific headline, a neighbor's tragic news, or a disturbing social media post, instead of feeling overwhelmed by the events you cannot control, why not inwardly declare, *Thank you beloved Universe for blessing these people with the gift of reverence. And so it is.* Even when the news is too emotionally unsettling for such a response, you can silently say to yourself, *Dear beloved Universe, please work through me to provide the gift of reverence for all involved. And so it is.* Notice how different life can be when you aren't carrying someone else's burden on your shoulders but simply acknowledging the next moment where the gift of reverence can be given.

- Since you may not always know who needs greater support or who is suffering in silence, aspire to use your new statement, "I am here with you," as the signature of each email or your parting words on a phone call.

CHAPTER 4

Anger Is a Reenactment of Someone Else's Trauma

s an empathic healer, holding space for other people's transformations can feel like being a doctor in a delivery room. While a person's spontaneous emotional surge puts them in a position to birth their next highest version of self, it often comes with a mixture of projections that a heart-centered person could quickly take personally.

Through this role and from a naturally merciful capacity, I was able to help others face pain, process trauma, and even revisit abuse. Conversely, when I wasn't working as a healer and was just an individual visiting with relatives during the holidays, I would notice my own jarring inner reactions to various family members. This dichotomy intrigued me. Why was I able to help total strangers process their deepest despair, while the patterning of my relatives still had the power to control me? I soon realized that the difference between my work and certain internal responses toward others was centered in how personally I interpreted their words and actions. As I recognized this, I began challenging myself to hold space for the healing of family members, especially when we gathered for the holidays.

With no need to take conversations beyond the realm of small talk, the process of holding space helped me see the healing underway. Since my family was unaware of the inner work happening among us, they continued to act out socially acceptable forms of unpleasant behavior that had previously felt like personal attacks against me.

The more I became aware of their healing journey—no matter how unaware they were of the transformations taking place—the less personally I took their actions. In the absence of feeling threatened by my family's behavior, I became more naturally interested in their lives. This helped me see how my family's defenses and judgments weren't personal. In fact, they had nothing to do with me. Instead of anticipating an inner countdown, waiting to see how long it would take for an interaction to trigger my own age-regressed behavior, I saw the moment from a more objective perspective. I clearly recognized how my family's reactions were less an attack on me and more a living testimony of their evolving journey.

Such a shift occurred during an encounter with a relative who asked me sarcastically whether being a healer was "even a career." I now had the capacity to recognize this comment from a more compassionate standpoint: they weren't making fun of me but sharing their own doubts about the nature of healing. I immediately softened in their presence and decided to answer as if they had taken a greater interest in my life. I replied, "That is such an honest question. I am quite blessed with the opportunity to help so many wonderful people. Thank you so much for asking. I appreciate your interest in my career."

My answer stumped them. I could tell they were only concerned with mindless chatter and blowing off steam from their daily stresses. But I wasn't attending a family gathering to be anyone's emotional punching bag or to be spoken to as if I were the child they remembered meeting many years ago. They asked me a question filled with sarcasm and judgment, but I decided to answer with earnestness. My response established them as an ally in my reality, no matter how cleverly their egos tried to instigate friction. While they spoke the language of inner conflict, I held the key role of speaking genuinely instead of defensively. No need to argue, point out anyone's judgmental behavior, or correct them from a more elusive position of righteousness. They had a right to be however they wished, and I, equally, had the power to decide how to interpret their words.

Of course, as I became more familiar with responding from a space-holding perspective, my opportunities for growth would only deepen through more intense interactions. While I was beginning to master small talk with relatives I only met at weddings, Bar Mitzvahs, and funerals, the real test would be adult encounters with a mother who always needed to get her way in order for her reality to feel stable.

Her patterning was such a confusing dance for me to see through. She would begin with constant requests for me to come visit my family for the holidays. No matter how busy my career had become, she often broke me down with guilt and coercion to give her what she wanted: the experience of her family being together. She would say, "You're always on tour. You can't take two days to see us?" Her words would play on my ability to stretch and conform to other people's demands just to keep the peace.

Finally, I would say, "Fine. It's only two days. I'll be there."

To deepen the manipulation, she would reply, "Please don't come if you don't want to." This caused me to prove to my mom that I really did want to come home, so she wouldn't see me as uncaring. It was the same power play I had fallen for my entire life.

No matter how many times I flew into town, the dance of patterning was always the same. First, a celebration: "Matthew is home!" both of my parents exclaimed as I walked in the door. Since I really loved my parents, I was genuinely happy to see them. Then we would sit on the couch and have a wonderfully connected conversation for about ten minutes. Soon, both would drift back toward the TV, which had been blaring an episode of *The People's Court* or *Judge Judy* at volume level 58.

That would leave me in amazement. I often thought, *I've been guilt-tripped into a visit and made to feel as if I'm a disconnected part of my family, only to sit on a living room couch and watch them do what they always do when I'm away?* I literally went from being the grand marshal of the welcome-home parade to a ghost in my childhood home observing my parents while they watched TV.

I even said to my mom, "Hey, how about we do something different and more interactive since I'm home for only a few days?"

"Oh, I just like having you here," she would respond. "I don't have to miss you when you visit."

While this was a sweet sentiment, it confused me. How could my mother spend so much time persuading me to fly home only to refuse to engage deeply with me once I arrived? I would hear her response and ultimately conclude, *If traveling across two state lines to watch court TV shows is how I can help her feel more of her son's love, then so be it.*

The next day, I joined my parents for a gathering at my sister's house. Here I would have the golden opportunity to test my space-holding skills in the presence of my mom's clever patterning. I remember bumping into her in my sister's kitchen after throwing away a paper plate of partially eaten appetizers. She asked me, "Are you coming back for the Bar Mitzvah in April?"

"I can't," I responded. "I'm leading a big five-day meditation retreat that month."

Instantly my mom's eyes darted fiercely toward me with a mixture of anger and disappointment. "You know, we don't ask for much. The least you could do is be a more active part of this family."

Since I had come to expect this kind of behavior, my mother's reaction didn't upset me. So I explained, "I set up my speaking schedule a year in advance. This is the first time I'm hearing of the Bar Mitzvah."

My strength melted a layer of her ego's mask to reveal a deeper intensity that knew how to crank up the heat of guilt when she didn't get her way. "I can't tell you how upset I am right now," she said, as her voice rose in exasperation.

Instead of caving in to her demands and defining my self-worth by her approval, I simply asked, "Why are you upset that I can't come when you don't even fully engage with me when I'm here?"

She looked at me with a glare that let me know her ego had no time for logic, facts, or reason. Through a clenched jaw, she said: "I just like having my family together. Is that okay with you?"

I didn't back down. "It's wonderful when we come together," I replied. "It reflects how life used to be. But it's not how it is anymore. We don't live together, and I'm no longer your little boy. If you feel my busy schedule is a rejection, I'm truly sorry that's how you interpret my choices."

Without missing a beat, my mom said, "I guess the old Jewish guilt doesn't work anymore, huh?"

I smiled. "Not on this man."

My mom walked toward me, gave me a hug, and let me know how proud she was of me. I told her that I was aware of how she felt her father had abandoned her.

She then asked me with curiosity, "How do you know I felt abandoned?"

"My whole life, I thought the words you projected at me were about my behavior," I explained. "But over time, I have come to see that your anger reveals the pain you haven't processed around your father. I use to feel so manipulated by your controlling actions. But then I realized you weren't really speaking to me but to a father from whom you wanted more attention. Those words were projected onto me as the perception of your absentee son.

I'm really sorry that your experience of your dad was so hurtful. I love you, Mom."

This was the moment when my mom met her adult son. It was also the moment I became immune to my family's manipulations. Now I could be with them and feel more open—not because they were any different but because the adult version of me had finally stepped forward. As I reflected further on this pivotal shift, I realized that the more I held space, the less personal other people's actions felt. The less personal each encounter seemed, the more merciful I was able to be.

The Attribute of Mercy

Mercy is how life appears when seen from the viewpoint of compassion. When mercy is present, we are keenly aware of the pain other people endure that causes them to be disconnected from their highest ethics and values. Through the attribute of mercy, you can depersonalize what may feel like tidal waves of blame battering the shoreline of your heart. When you understand emotional triggers as a road map leading your awareness back to early, painful experiences, you will become more compassionate toward the inability most people have to face their own deep vulnerabilities. When ego remains active as a force of unconsciousness, we tend to interpret other people's actions by how they affect us personally. This level of perception often sees reality from a self-referencing standpoint: *What does this have to do with me? Why is this happening to me? How come this always happens to me?*

The questions that maintain a self-referencing perspective provide you with little space to develop a greater awareness of other people's struggles. In essence, just because it's happening to you, doesn't mean it's actually about you. Equally so, anything happening in your sphere of reality is sure to create growth in your evolution.

The more time you spend holding space for your own healing, the more your ego softens to surrender its fight for control. This allows you to remain relaxed in your body and centered in truth.

Think about my mother's situation. Her lashing out and manipulative behavior toward me for abandoning her really had little to do with me. Rather she projected onto me the words and attitudes she had not directed to the real source of her pain—her father. This brings me to the deeper truth: *anger represents the words someone never spoke to those who hurt them the most.*

Undoubtedly, it can be painful to be on the receiving end of someone's projected emotions. This is why holding space for anger as the reenactment of someone's trauma takes time, patience, and practice. More than likely, this process will occur incrementally. It may require you to excuse yourself from tumultuous encounters and hold private space for yourself, especially if your sensitivities are triggered. But with time, attention, and dedication, the many attributes you are cultivating, including mercy, will deepen the beauty of intimate connection for everyone's mutual benefit.

What Could Possibly Go Wrong?

While not fair or pleasant in any way, it is common to unconsciously project our anger onto people we perceive as safe. Just as nurses may hear abusive statements hurled in their direction when someone is in intense pain, as a sacred space holder, it is helpful for you to interpret the words that express someone else's discomfort to be about them instead of you.

However, no matter how pure anyone's intention may be, holding space is never a justification for tolerating any form of abuse. While each person's nervous system has its own threshold of intensity, it's our responsibility to ensure we're holding space to the degree that we can handle. Since anger is a reenactment of someone's trauma, it's crucial to explore a few key scenarios of what could possibly go wrong.

Despite the demands of each person's ego, people only deserve the amount of time you are willing to authentically share. If you feel pressured into giving someone time and energy you don't have, conforming to their demands will put you in a position you may be unable to handle emotionally. Even if that person gives you an ultimatum that you must attend to their needs or risk losing them, you should always follow the authority of your own inner guidance. It knows what options are best for you, and knowing what is best for you is equally beneficial for the evolution of all. Despite the pressure others may project, you're always better off creating space for more genuine people than succumbing to manipulative tactics of those who fill your life with more egos to appease. Just because somebody needs to reenact their traumas through layers of anger, it doesn't mean you have to be the one to witness it.

When choosing to do so, you might hold space for a depth of anger you know has nothing to do with you, while the person projecting their feelings remains convinced that you're the source of all of their suffering. This may trigger the righteousness of your own inner rescuer who will try to free you from the intensity of their false accusations by correcting every misperception.

If you're able to remain safe in your body, you may explore what happens when you witness an angry person without being overwhelmed by their projections. The more you can hold this kind of merciful space, the calmer you'll be while listening. The more you are able to listen openly, the less the frenzy of their debate will trigger opposition in you. This can deescalate the intensity of the conflict. While never a guarantee, viewing someone's inner conflict through the attribute of mercy may invite the angry person to become more aware of how exhausted they feel by remaining attached to the argument they insist on winning.

You may even be holding space for your life partner who doesn't know how to share vulnerable feelings without assigning blame. While you might recognize that their feelings are rooted in memories of earlier authority figures, they may not. Their self-referencing ego may decide that the nature of their conflict pertains to issues with you that were already resolved, including details you can't even remember.

Whether you're the person being projected upon or the person doing the projecting, holding space gives you the opportunity to share feelings freely without assigning blame. When both people are equipped with this skill set, sharing occurs through the give and take of listening with encouragement, responding with validation, complimenting with reverent perspective, and witnessing from a space of mercy.

While you don't have to do another person's inner work, one of the reasons you exist in their life is to simply put them on notice when their words and behavior become too much to bear. This doesn't make you weak, less than, low vibrational, a negative person, or an example of victimhood. It celebrates your willingness to be true to yourself, honoring exactly where you are in your path and all that you need to thrive and shine. This occurs without you treating yourself as a concept of perfectionism that has nothing to do with the inherent perfection of authenticity always alive within you.

Holding space for people who have a subconscious fear of rejection may cause them to lash out so intensely, it ensures that you'll inevitably leave. This will confirm how worthless they feel about themselves, while acting out a self-fulfilling prophecy: the reaction they want the least is the one most likely to occur based on their behavior. Rather than gutting it out and trying to prove that their subconscious beliefs are wrong, always make sure you don't confuse overgiving with attentiveness.

As you learn this difference, you will be able to see quite clearly how the purpose of holding space is to create an environment of mutual safety, so everyone may be seen and heard. If anyone is being mistreated, this sacred ground has been breached, requiring a momentary or permanent form of distance for the greater good of all. It may not be the option you or anyone else wants, but it will always be the very thing everyone needs for the healing that is underway.

Setting an Intention for Mercy

To release the ego's fight for control and hold a space of mercy for yourself and others, please repeat the following words out loud:

I intend to hold space through the attribute of mercy for myself and others beyond my ego's desire to fight for something to control. I allow the attribute of mercy to be offered from a space of restraint, as an offering of surrender for the liberation of all. I recognize the attribute of mercy as a gift I am free to share when I desire to hold space for another and never when coerced by the demands of another person's ego. I intend to remember that whenever blame, threat, or accusation is projected in my direction to the degree that I feel overwhelmed or fear for my safety, the most merciful response is ending the interaction to find a safer environment to hold space for me. While someone else may insist they're being abandoned, I accept that sometimes another person's deepest breakthroughs may come to be only in my absence. If such volatility continues, I embrace my responsibility to enact greater boundaries, even permanently, so as not to put myself in danger through the mercy I am showing another.

In knowing it is so, I allow the attribute of mercy to support the redemption of all, no matter how it's received, overlooked, or denied, or whether I agree with the viewpoints of any personal sharing. If and when this hurts my feelings, triggers memories of past traumas, makes me more distrusting of others, or causes me to shut down in rejection or lash out in resentment, I allow myself the sacred space to be with my feelings and offer the gift of mercy to any part of me. Whether given to myself or another person or as an active blessing to humanity, I welcome the attribute of mercy to reveal a renewed depth of compassion that may not match the requests of anyone's demands but shall always be exactly what is needed for greater transformation to emerge. And so it is.

The Supportive Statement of Mercy

"I Now See How You've Been Mistreated"

No matter where the finger of blame points, through the attribute of mercy, you're able to hold space for eruptions of anger. If you can be an objective witness, you make it acceptable for others to share hurtful feelings for as long as you feel safe and able to do so. Equally so, the more often you hold space for your own defensiveness, the more comfortable you will feel when others act out the same patterns. Of course, there is an invisible line that can't be crossed where the tendency to blame becomes abusive. Because such a boundary is different for each individual, you can only hold authentic space for as long as that boundary isn't crossed to your own detriment.

In most cases, people will require a few moments to cry, shake, plead, and blame just to move the energy erupting from within them. For the one holding space, the attribute of mercy contains the wisdom to honor someone's history of experience without personalizing the narratives they may project. This is why one of the most merciful statements you can make in response to an expression of anger is "Based on what you've shared, I now see how you've been mistreated."

Whether someone treats you the way another person treated them in the past, demonstrates the hurtful ways an authority figure behaved, reenacts with you the dynamic their parents played out, or shows you exactly how their inner critic ebbs and flows in their own mind, most accusations are never the fault of a space holder. They're simply the product of a person's unconscious tendency to blame or mistreat the one they feel the safest around. They do this because people always find safety in the presence of someone who embodies more of the heart-centeredness they are working toward achieving.

Even while this may be true, there is no justification for abusive behavior. But the more you become aware of anger as a reenactment of someone's trauma, the less threatened you are likely to feel. Even though others may feel safer letting out their deeper feelings with you as their witness, you're never required to play such a role unless it's a space you agree to hold. This is why all you can do is be clear in your words, actions, and intentions, while having the inner strength to allow others the right to their own experience.

If someone's complaint actually carries validity, the clarity of your inner knowing will politely tap you on the shoulder and invite a deeper look into the subtle motivations lurking in your behavior. For the most part, though, each complaint that comes your way is an inner child's primal attempt to articulate the hardship of despair, where the healing isn't dependent upon anything that's said but the depth of emotion each statement can release. This is why, whether motivated to stay or inspired to go, we end difficult encounters through the inner knowing of mercy, meeting any personal struggle with the renewed awareness: "Based on what you've shared, I now see how you've been mistreated."

Mercy in Action

Through the attribute of mercy, you are better able to directly notice the heartache of unfairness that each person carries within.

Perhaps you are a witness to a friend's or relative's endless complaints about being at odds with their partner. If you are acting as an objective observer of their experience instead of joining them in their blame, they may accuse you of secretly siding with their partner, especially if you're unwilling to take their side. By recognizing their anger as a reenactment of trauma, you are holding a merciful space to inspire their deeper feelings and bring more truthful perspectives to the surface.

What if an angry boss or manipulative coworker views the workplace as the only environment in which their ego has any semblance of control? While it's no measure of success to endure the effects of toxic environments, from a less personal perspective, you can clearly see how their ego often picks at the insecurities and doubts of those who shine brightly. What if your ability to simply observe their hurtful actions as a window into the pain they refuse to process allows the attribute of mercy to be the best protection against their problem with you?

Maybe in moments of generosity, when you are called to offer money to a homeless person, you also ask their name and let them know what a pleasure it is to meet them. All too often, the deepest personal losses, unhealed traumas, and patterns of addiction can be among the many circumstances causing someone to spiral into the harshest climate of survival—leaving people stripped of their dignity, especially when their fellow human beings ignore them. Whether or not you are inspired to give any money, why not also donate a moment of your time to let them know they're seen, heard, and valued? What if that simple moment of mercy inspires a series of actions that transforms a homeless person into a rehabilitated citizen and successful business owner?

Perhaps a salesperson's short-tempered demeanor doesn't require you to complain to the manager. Maybe a scathing online review is more likely to feed your ego's self-righteousness than elicit tangible change. What if that person's negative attitude becomes your moment of merciful respect for the hardships they must have endured or continue to face in order to replay trauma in the way they're behaving?

What if you become aware of how you are reenacting trauma at other people's expense through outbursts of anger? Perhaps you've taken out on your children your hostility toward your ex? What if disappointments at work over which you had no control leave you short-tempered toward those you love? What if instead of judging yourself for acting out, you openly acknowledge your behavior, apologize to those you've hurt, and recognize the space you need so that the lingering pain you carry will harm no one else?

Mercy as a Daily Practice

To bring the attribute of mercy to the forefront of your awareness, try one or all of these daily practices:

- Whenever you judge someone for their behavior or criticize their perceptions, take a moment to replace any label you project onto them with a greater awareness of their unhealed pain. May you exchange *jerk, enemy,* or an expletive-laden slur with the recognition that they're a suffering person who is unjustly taking out their inner conflict on others. In honor of the space you hold for everyone to heal, may you turn toward their unhealed wounds with merciful empathy rather than hide from them behind a wall of judgment.

- Please take a moment to consider the depth of heartbreak, trauma, or abandonment a person who has hurt you must have experienced in order to cause you harm. You may even visualize that person and say to their image, "Based on how you've mistreated me, I now see how you've been mistreated."

- Try the practice that's affectionately known as "the barf bucket." It begins when a person who has emotions to purge asks someone else, "Are you able to hold space for me?" If so, the space holder metaphorically creates a container of safety for the words the person needs to spew in order to move the energy erupting inside.

This practice establishes a space of mindfulness where any expression of blame, fear masquerading as accusation, and beliefs in victimhood can minimize the chance that a space holder's feelings are hurt. It's also a way for each person to learn that what needs to be said may be a valid way to voice pain, but it doesn't also mean that the content being shared is of the highest truth. Even when no one is around to hold the barf bucket for you, you can always hold it for yourself as you speak out loud or write in a journal the words you need to share.

CHAPTER 5

When Someone Fights Their Pain, You Get Pushed Away

efore I began my career as an empathic healer, I was a personal trainer. It was the unlikeliest of career paths since I had little athletic experience, I grew up with severe asthma, and I never played sports or did anything strenuous. As a child who was always fascinated with superheroes, I secretly dreamed of the day I would go from being the smallest kid in class to a super buff, larger-than-life character. That was the fantasy at least. Little did I know how close I'd come to living it out.

During high school, classmates with physical conditions like mine were put into a program called adaptive PE. Rather than run laps like most kids had to do, a handful of us were gathered to engage in gentle forms of exercise.

But one day, the PE teacher told us, "Starting today and twice a week for the remainder of the year, we'll meet in the weight room." I thought to myself with a sense of excitement, *Where all the athletes train?* For one of the first times in my life, the notion of physical exertion excited me.

I kept envisioning *The Incredible Hulk*, a popular TV series in the '80s. My favorite part was always near the end of each episode when Bill Bixby's character, Dr. David Banner, would transform into the Incredible Hulk (played by bodybuilding legend, Lou Ferrigno) and take down his enemies.

I really gravitated toward weight training. We started with very light dumbbells and would exchange them for heavier ones if we could perform a lift with perfect form. Surprisingly, the lighter ones didn't seem so heavy as I marveled at the physical strength I never knew I had. This set ablaze in me a new-found passion that led to my parents buying me a membership at the local YMCA. Soon I moved up to a big-box gym where a personal trainer mentored me. He was much like an older brother. He designed my programs as well as an eating regimen. At this point, I was seventeen years old.

After lifting weights regularly for about eight months, I grew from 98 pounds to 165 pounds of muscle packed onto a five-foot-tall frame. I even remember one fateful day when I went to Gold's Gym in Venice Beach, California. In the world of bodybuilding, this was the mecca of weightlifting. In celebration of my passion and the transformation I was undergoing, I put on my most coveted training gear and bought a guest pass. The gym was huge—like a warehouse of intensity. It was one of the coolest places I'd ever visited.

As soon as I walked in, I saw three or four professional body-builders whose physiques had inspired my continual drive to train. For someone with this interest, it was like walking the red carpet at the Oscars. I even saw a photo shoot in the corner of the gym for an upcoming issue of *Flex* magazine. I was almost having an out-of-body experience.

At this point, I grabbed some weights and started doing bi-cep curls. I had developed the ability to hold a sixty-five-pound dumbbell in each hand and lift with slow precise form. As I set both dumbbells down, I saw out of the corner of my eye someone sitting on the adjacent bench watching me. I turned and nearly passed out. It was Lou Ferrigno! The Incredible Hulk I had idolized as a kid was smiling and giving me a thumbs-up. Holy the-you-know-what! I shook his hand, let him know how much I loved his show, and kept lifting, so as not to make it weird. *Relax Matt. Just act like you belong here*, I told myself. In such a surreal way, I did belong there. It was one of the few times in my life I had felt a sense of connection in a community setting. For at least those few hours at Gold's Gym, I knew that these were my people. It instilled greater confidence in me and helped me feel a sense of personal value. I understood that I had something to contribute to this world.

Soon after, I completed a certification course and began working as a personal trainer. During this time, I met a client who would quickly become my workout partner and best friend. I became a mentor to him just like I'd had a mentor when I began lifting.

It wasn't until I encountered some rather unexpected adversities that our bond began to shift. I remember spotting a client during a rather simple lift when I felt a weird sensation in my lower back. It didn't really hurt; it just felt odd. The very next day, I woke up in excruciating sciatic pain—any degree of movement sent surges of electricity down my spine. After a few X-rays, my doctor diagnosed two bulging discs that were pressing against my spinal cord. He put me on prescription pain medication and weekly epidural shots of cortisone. I even had to move back in with my parents since I could no longer work and had limited mobility.

During this difficult time, my intuitive abilities began to blossom. My best friend would visit me, and I would spontaneously channel information about his experiences and family dynamic. This ultimately resulted in my life taking an incredible turn toward spirituality.

But all was not well. After about a year, I said to my doctor, "I'm really tired of taking these pills. They don't take away my pain. They just make me not care about the pain I'm in. I can't live like this."

The doctor's response: "You've been on this powerful medication for a long time, so you can't just stop cold turkey."

"So I'll wean myself off," I suggested.

"You have to do so in a medical rehabilitation facility to ensure that it's done safely," he explained.

My jaw hit the floor. "I have to go to rehab? I'm not abusing these drugs. I've simply followed all your directions."

Throwing his hands in the air, he replied, "I'm sorry Matt. This is just the way it works."

So, there I was, less than forty-eight hours later, admitted into rehab, not knowing why this was "just the way it works." Every few hours, a nurse gave me a concoction of pills to ease my detox symptoms. I was furious. *I don't want more pills. I don't want any pills. Get me out of here!* I thought.

With each day in rehab, my intuitive abilities amplified, so I passed the time giving readings to people around me. I became a circus attraction—which was fine with me, as it took my mind off having to spend thirty days in a facility where people with true addiction issues endured their grueling process.

On day twenty-seven of my thirty-day program, it was time for friends and family to visit. When my parents and best friend entered the facility, it was such a refreshing reminder of the life that awaited me outside those walls. Still, I was emotionally raw, and for my best friend, this was an unfamiliar version of me. I had always been the one with all the answers and my life in order. At first I felt his encouragement, but soon I had to support him through his big leap of trying to support me during one of my most difficult moments of despair.

I broke down. "I can't be here anymore," I cried. "This place is hell. Please get me the fuck out of here!" I pleaded.

My best friend tried to level with me: "It's only three more days."

"I can't do it! You don't understand what it's like in here!" I wasn't mad at him. I was just so done with an experience that wasn't quite done with me.

Soon, visiting hours were over. I wasn't hostile or physically violent in any way, but I'd had one of the deepest emotional breakdowns I'd ever experienced. As my parents and best friend left, I noticed a rather startled look on his face. He had tried to support me for a brief moment, but when it didn't seem to help, he just shut down. I could see in his eyes that he was frightened of my emotional state. And, for the first time in our friendship, I couldn't rescue him from his discomfort.

After completing my thirty-day program, I said to the Universe, *I'm done. If you heal my back, I will serve your will.* After declaring such words from a space of incredible desperation, I suddenly felt a shift. The intense pain I'd grown accustomed to living with had disappeared. This actually startled me because I couldn't believe that what I'd asked for had unfolded immediately. This was the moment when everything I needed in order to serve others as a healer started falling into place.

Once back home, I would reach out to my best friend regularly, but he had become profoundly avoidant. It seemed rather difficult just to make plans, which always fell through. Finally, one afternoon, we met for lunch. When he arrived and sat across from me, his eyes projected daggers of piercing anger bordering on hostility. I shared with him the advances I was making in my career as a healer, but all I could sense from him was his desire to get away from me.

It seemed as if my time in rehab had robbed him of the person I had been in his life. His inability to handle my moment of emotional duress shattered his image of who I was to him. He now regarded me as a person who had stolen his best friend and personal mentor. But I was sitting directly in front of him, wondering where on Earth my best friend had gone.

When I ordered lunch and he didn't, I knew in my gut this would be the last time I would see him. Even though I was the one feeling abandonment and betrayal from such a shift in our connection, I mercifully sensed he couldn't handle this degree of realness. I offered a humble smile as if to thank him for being a part of my life and the opportunity to be a part of his journey. And then I said, "Well . . . "

This led to one of those awkward pauses that, ironically, felt quite comfortable to me. His walls of anger started to lower, as I could see tears gathering in his eyes. But he quickly composed himself and said, "I gotta go." This would be the last time I ever saw or heard from the best friend I thought I had. I was devastated.

Despite this great loss, I continued immersing myself in my healing work. But behind the persona of a psychic superhero initially driven to rescue others from their despair, there existed a disappointed heart that had accepted the role of service as a way of not letting anyone in deeply enough to cause devastation again. Thankfully, this wasn't my ultimate resting place, but it would be where I would remain while processing the sadness of my friend's pain pushing me away.

As each piece of my heart came back together in wholeness, I began holding space for even deeper shifts of healing by outgrowing some of my rescuer tendencies. In retrospect, it was an inevitable transition unexpectedly inspired by my best friend's disappearance. He had become so dependent on my help—just as I had become dependent on helping him—that I had overlooked the chance to teach him how to serve himself.

The Attribute of Worthiness

Through the attribute of worthiness, you are compassionately aware of the healing that comes and goes throughout someone's life. Their tendencies to withdraw, reject, and abandon become evidence of the pain they are going through—a pain that can be projected onto you even when you're trying to lovingly hold space for the healing underway. Even with the best of intentions, you may be criticized, rejected, or abandoned as a way for others to avoid the pain they feel. The more you're able to see other people's behavior as more about their experience than your actions, the more your self-worth remains intact without you becoming an emotional doormat for them to walk on.

As your sense of worthiness amplifies, you will notice the natural rhythm of life. No matter how it plays out, we are free to recognize that everything that comes inevitably goes; anything gained is sure to be lost; each experience of birth foreshadows an equal experience of death. Along the way, the prime motivation of ego seeks to control reality, hoping each beginning, birth, and gain can somehow come without each inevitable loss. But because one side of experience can't exist without the other, the ego's motivation is a fantasy—a delusion that it can find a way to control reality. The more holding space deepens throughout your healing journey, the more likely it will be that your ego stops fighting to control a reality where change is the only likely outcome.

As you recognize this process of ego unraveling, you'll honor the alone time people need. This is more a necessity for their journey than who does or doesn't accept you, even when the only way someone knows how to ask for the space they are unaware they need is by pushing you away.

There are moments in life when others will benefit from your presence, giving their mirror neurons the opportunity to attune to your heart-centered frequency. In other instances, your presence may trigger uncomfortable feelings that are unrelated to your behavior. It may even cause others to reject you due to the emotions they're intent on denying. For example, you may sit down with your partner, a friend, or family member to discuss the ways in which the relationship feels stagnant, one-sided, or out of balance. If they carry a history where accountability was associated with a punishment handed down by a parent or authority figure, they may dismiss the merit of the discussion or even accuse you of judging them. This occurs as their soul's way of saying, *This body is too overwhelmed processing past trauma on a subconscious level to remain open in your presence. While you are a gift in my life, you are currently a distraction from the feelings you have brought up for me to experience. This is why I am pushing you away, even if I am not consciously aware of it or able to put it into words.*

All the while, your inner child may translate this request for space to mean: *I'm not enough. I wasn't perfect enough, otherwise they wouldn't have rejected me.* Without a need to correct its vulnerable perspective or accept it as the highest truth in existence, the necessity of holding space allows each feeling to be valid from our inner child's viewpoint. This may help you see moments of rejection as subconscious requests for space without feeding the belief that you are less than, unworthy, or inferior. Through the attribute of worthiness, you can respect each person's healing journey, while taking greater responsibility for your own feelings, especially if the light of your presence seems more overwhelming than soothing to others.

When witnessing someone's pain is no longer a trauma for you to process, you will have successfully stepped into greater alignment with the attribute of worthiness. The more time you spend choosing to hold space over turning other people's needs against yourself, the greater your capacity will be to move through each emotional wave with peace, openness, and ease.

Whether giving someone space helps them to return as a more mature expression of self or signals the end of the relationship you had hoped would go so much further, you are cultivating the power to move with the rhythm of change, with empowerment versus imprisonment. This occurs when you are rooted in self-worth as you hold space for the evolving worth of others—even if the only way another person knows how to meet themselves on a deeper level is by pushing others away.

What Could Possibly Go Wrong?

When someone pushes you away because they don't know how to ask for the space they need, your reaction will depend on your threshold of tolerance, your expectations, and what you are or aren't willing to endure. Even though it is natural to desire being there for others, perhaps in a way that people from their past couldn't be there for them, authentic space holding doesn't blossom from codependency—as if you have to stay the course in every relationship and wear it as a badge of honor no matter how painful the dynamic may be. Many in this world grew up with the model of codependency as a misguided example of loyalty and dedication. *We will get through this together*, is certainly an honorable notion, as long as circumstances can bring people together rather than tear them apart. But if experiences that stir unprocessed trauma are entry points for greater spiritual evolution, your unwavering code of empowered conduct must remain active to ensure that no one takes out their frustrations on you.

While in previous chapters I've highlighted examples of what could go wrong when others react to your heart-centered support, in this section, we will address a painful misstep that occurs when you confuse people pleasing and codependency with unconditional love.

Loving someone unconditionally never means giving them permission to treat you poorly or blame their behavior on stress while you live as their disempowered caretaker. While overwhelming feelings can cause people in your life to shut down emotionally and no longer act as the happy-go-lucky characters you met initially, there is a difference between digging deep throughout moments of adversity and using the stresses of life as an excuse to hurt or control you when discomfort or frustration surface.

One of the biggest mistakes I've seen in relationships—especially for those steeped in a spiritual journey—occurs when people use acceptance, forgiveness, and unconditional love as excuses to stay in toxic relationships when it's really their wound of unworthiness that prevents them from leaving. It's quite common for the vibration of fear to lurk in misguided forms of spiritual justification, whether someone legitimately fears for their personal safety, imagines that a breakup isn't "what the Universe wants me to do" unless their partner agrees, or simply dreads they'll never find a better match. As victims of toxicity, manipulation, or abuse wait for the "right time" to act bravely, there can be no clearer exit sign than moments of mistreatment.

When you express unconditional love through the attribute of worthiness, there's nothing you and others can't overcome, especially if you come together in the equality and solidarity of unity consciousness. In order for this deep empowerment to occur, each person must agree to respect themselves and those around them, no matter how intensely the inevitability of change has entered their lives. While some days will naturally be harder than others, there's never a time when the only relief for the stress of an unexpectedly grueling day is to punish, judge, or control another. Even when someone's anger as the reenactment of trauma gives you a direct view into how they've been mistreated, healing occurs when you break the cycles of abuse by daring to be more honorable than the egregious actions of people who have done harm.

No long-lasting healing can occur until you've established boundaries, especially when abuse, disrespect, or manipulation surface. The notion that someone who is afraid of conflict can hide from reality in a room decorated with prayer flags, candles, and incense, while attempting to "accept what is," highlights one of the most insidious misuses of spiritual wisdom. If the true aim of "accepting what is" is your goal, then you will accept any mistreatment as a sign of completion for those who only know how to hurt others in response to the hurt people have inflicted on them. If unconditional love is your highest value, then please remember you can't show loving support to another person when you remain complacent and complicit in toxic patterning.

This is especially true if children are involved. The time you spend operating as an accessory to someone else's abusive tactics teaches kids' subconscious minds to normalize this kind of damaging environment. They will define toxic dynamics as how adults are supposed to behave and even model the beliefs that domination, manipulation, and abuse are how they get what they want from others.

As you continue to become a source of unconditionally loving support for your own inner child, please also make sure that the fear that emanates from your youngest broken parts doesn't influence decisions that hold you, others, or even innocent children captive to the self-serving patterning of someone else's ego. For example, let's say you are in a relationship with an individual whose emotional patterning or escalating addictions creates a hostile living environment for you and your children. While your intuition says, *It's time to go*, you interpret it as a judgment about that person's shortcomings, assume you will be damaging your kids' lives by breaking up their home, or even fear that your partner will take their own life without you continuing as an enabler of their toxic patterning. All the while, a willingness to stay keeps you stuck, while subconsciously teaching your children that the dynamic they are recording in the memory of their cells is an example of a healthy and normal relationship.

This may help you see what could go wrong when the harm or rejection caused by someone else's pain has less to do with your behavior and more to do with their unconscious reactions becoming repetitive patterns of abuse. Through the attribute of worthiness, when you refuse to compromise the integrity of your own worth and value, you will manifest connections that no heart can deny.

Setting an Intention for Worthiness

To release the enabling qualities that justify abuse and hold a space of worthiness for yourself and others, please repeat the following words out loud:

I intend to hold space through the attribute of worthiness for myself and others without taking out my pain on anyone else or justifying the ways others may hide from pain by mistreating me. I allow worthiness to be offered from a space of assertive clarity, as an offering of empowerment for the maturity of all. I recognize the attribute of worthiness as a gift I am free to share, as it helps me recognize the space people need when pushed away, rejected, or abandoned by the pain another person processes. Instead of trying to prove my value and importance to someone needing space, I accept the equal benefit I provide, whether offered in my presence or better received in my absence. No matter the feelings that such a need for space triggers, I acknowledge it as an opportunity to commune with my own innocence on a deeper level to inspire greater expressions of worthiness in me. As a sacred space holder, I allow the enabling qualities that justify abuse to be cleared out of my energy field, returned to the source of its origin, transmuted completely, and healed to completion now.

In knowing it is so, I allow the attribute of worthiness to support the softening of all, no matter how it's received, overlooked, or denied, or whether I agree with the viewpoints of any personal sharing. If and when this hurts my feelings, triggers memories of past traumas, makes me more distrusting of others, or causes me to shut down in rejection or lash out in resentment, I allow myself the sacred space to be with my feelings and offer the gift of worthiness to any unworthy part of me. Whether given to myself or another person or as an active blessing to humanity, I allow the attribute of worthiness to support my decision-making with more courage instead of complacency from this moment forward. And so it is.

The Supportive Statement of Worthiness

"Thank You for Helping Me Understand the Space You Need"

Through the attribute of worthiness, you neither turn other people's reactions into a disempowering story about yourself nor tolerate how they lash out when the heat of adversity is turned up in their lives. Much like a wounded animal hiding in anticipation of looming predators, when someone fights their own pain, they push others away. While you may not embody the predatory qualities of a person's past trauma, their subconscious mind can associate you with it and perceive you as a potential threat. This is why giving space is always as important as holding space. Others may not recognize how much space they need or even want to be alone with their feelings. Yet, this becomes astoundingly clear once the attribute of worthiness helps you be supportive of their innocence while also refusing to tolerate abusive tendencies.

With the supportive statement "Thank you for helping me understand the space you need," you neutralize the sting of rejection by acknowledging the gift of space you can offer others for their journey.

Even when you're the one needing space, the supportive statement can shift to suggest "Thank you for helping me understand the space I need" so as not to project your feelings on a loved one. If you're unable to ask for space or honor the space someone else needs, this codependent patterning only sets the stage for more enmeshed behavior and dynamics of unconsciousness. Sometimes in life, you personify love as the heart someone else embraces. At other times, you are asked to be the love that wants so much goodness for another person, you're willing to step out of their way if that's what it takes for them to move toward greater happiness.

Even when someone's demand for space turns into adultery, betrayal, deception, or abandonment, you're better off accepting the loss of this partnership by acknowledging the true motives of their character than to remain unaware and potentially subjected to far worse treatment.

Whether in response to a partner who has deceived you or a friend who withdraws when life gets difficult or disappears from your life when they enter into a romantic relationship or even to someone associating you with their own history of pain, the supportive statement "Thank you for helping me understand the space you need" releases the past, helps you hold space from afar, and makes the fulfillment of your own needs a more consistent focus for the worthiness you deserve.

Worthiness in Action

Through the attribute of worthiness, you embody love from a standpoint of empowerment, instead of being an emotional punching bag for others.

Perhaps you are open to being available to someone in their dire hour of pain, grief, and uncertainty. No matter how impeccable your intentions may be, what if your very presence acts as a distraction, preventing them from really diving into their feelings because they've become preoccupied by their fear of how you'll judge their most vulnerable parts? Even when you attempt to convince them of how accepting you are, can you see this as an opportunity to give them the gift of space instead of fighting to maintain the role you've played in their lives up until now?

What if you perceive your children's aggressive behavior as an inability to cope with the inevitable changes and losses in life and not proof that you're an incompetent parent failing your mission? What if through the offering of space, you give your children time to know themselves better, so they're more open to sharing the details of their experiences at a later time? What if the space you give doesn't mean they're spending more time suffering but is reflective of how young impressionable minds come to terms with who they are and how they feel?

Maybe you can interpret the rejection of a lover as the best-case scenario for what life has prepared both of you to receive? Maybe the distance or absence of someone you imagined spending your life with frees you both from potential mistreatment and toxic entanglement?

What if fate created the circumstance that caused you to be unable to say goodbye to a relative on their deathbed? Maybe they required the time and space to be alone in order to let go into the afterlife instead of being distracted by the loved ones they were afraid to leave? What if it was never your fault for missing their final breath but exactly how their passing needed to unfold for the greater good of everyone's journey?

Perhaps you haven't been pushed away by a friend's pain but from the joy they found in a new romantic partner. Are you able to support their new love, even when it seems like a dear friend may be less available to connect with you?

Worthiness as a Daily Practice

To bring the attribute of worthiness to the forefront of your awareness, try one or all of these daily practices:

- This practice helps you be more in tune with your feelings instead of deepening beliefs of disempowerment when someone's need for space pushes you away. Notice how with each of the five steps, this process escorts you into a greater space of worthiness and awareness. Simply fill each of the blanks with an emotion that best describes how you felt in response to someone else's need for space. Then read each one slowly to internalize each shift:

    a. I'm feeling _____ because of other people's actions.

  b. I'm feeling _____ because I'm feeling _____ and not because of other people's actions.

  c. Other people's actions help me see the unresolved patterns of _____ that linger inside of me.

  d. I'm grateful for the opportunity to heal _____ at a deeper level.

  e. Thank you to everyone who is helping me heal _____ for the benefit and well-being of all.

- Just as you would instruct a child who senses danger, if you are being mistreated, feel threatened, or have been harmed, it's of the utmost importance that you inform the trusted people in your life. Since one of the most important steps in breaking cycles of abuse is to overcome tendencies to defend the abuser despite threats or manipulations, it's essential to let a loved one or even the local authorities know when it occurs. No matter how low or unworthy of help you feel, or how little you trust the inner workings of the legal system, the only way for true healing to occur is when you are no longer a distraction for the controlling patterns of an abuser's ego. If you're unsure whether the actions are abusive or wonder if you may be perceiving them through a lens of unprocessed trauma, please seek the advice of a licensed, well-trained therapist who will provide the objective perspective you need.

- May the simplest actions of inspired empowerment allow you to step forward into greater self-worth every day. Whether it's decluttering the garage, reorganizing a closet, or making time for musical interests or other creative ambitions, may you take time to prove to yourself how different today is from any yesterday before. No matter how much defensiveness your ego projects, it's worth every degree of effort to remember that you are worthy of the change that can only transform your life for the better.

CHAPTER 6

Diversity Is the Guiding Light of Compassion

I remember the day distinctly. The sky seemed ominous, as if it were using all of its strength to brace the world for a moment of impact. It's a feeling similar to the one I experienced when I was in the schoolyard, moments before a fight broke out, or the calm before the storm reminiscent of the Los Angeles riots that occurred in 1992, after the Rodney King verdict was announced. I turned on my TV and saw on several different stations a law enforcement officer kneeling on a man's neck. The man was in pain, struggling to breathe, pleading for his life, even calling out for his mother. What happened? Why were four officers using this much force in such a casual way for a sustained period of time?

After nine horrendous minutes, the officers took the life of George Floyd in a misuse of power that occurred in broad daylight. I was shocked, confused, and horrified as I watched Minneapolis, along with so many other cities across the country, come unglued. Unlike the LA riots that I couldn't really comprehend or process at such a young age, this time I had no emotional distance while observing this outpouring of rage. It felt as if the civil unrest I was witnessing was occurring inside me; each part of my body burning with anger as cities were set ablaze. I distinctly remember the prayer I kept reciting: *May all that is occurring unfold for the well-being of all.* It had become one of my most mature prayers. Instead of trying to oppose expressions of violence already underway, I set an intention for greater harmony, well-being, and equality to rise from the ashes of all that was crumbling.

For me, this was a life-changing experience. I had always supported equal rights for all beings, embracing the peaceful and inspiring messages of my childhood heroes like Dr. Martin Luther King, Jr., and Gandhi. I always stood up for other kids being bullied in school and enjoyed friendships with those from a wide range of ethnicities. I fondly remember as a kid hanging out with a friend whose family was of Middle Eastern descent. After hours of playing video games, I would secretly hope his mom would make us a plate of delicious Persian rice that was unlike the standard American diet I'd grown accustomed to eating.

As a passionate supporter of racial equality, I was mesmerized as I watched waves of unrest break out across the country. Then, names I had never heard before began circulating: Manuel "Mannie" Elijah Ellis, William Howard Green, Breonna Taylor, Daniel T. Prude, Michael Brent Ramos, Dreasjon "Sean" Reed. Now, George Perry Floyd. And the list continues.

These were only a few of the people who had been tragically killed by members of law enforcement whom I had been taught to honor as pillars of the community and symbols of safety. Having grown up with friends whose parents patrolled the streets, I had always idealized the image of police. As a kid, just the mere sight of a squad car or pair of officers walking the local mall infused me with a sense of relief. On the other hand, many people

I knew, whose ethnicity was different from mine, had far scarier experiences whenever the police showed up.

As a kid, I comprehended the idea of systemic racism from a space of unintentional distance. My heart would ache anytime I saw or heard about mistreatment, but it always felt like a *Sorry this happened to you* type of response. When I was younger, I thought that gesture was sensitive, compassionate, and humble, which at the time was very much the space it had come from in me.

But this situation felt different. It seemed like a collective karmic blowout for generations of repressed pain and overlooked hardship toward my fellow human beings.

Whenever current events unfold for a moment of collective healing, I always use my social media platform as a way of promoting unity, peace, and love. That day, a great pause came over me. Am I the best spokesperson for this moment? Would I be taking away an opportunity from someone of a different race to step forward and lead peacefully? Was peace even what these times called for, given the amount of criminal abuse perpetrated against others that I would never experience? What is this moment truly asking of me?

No matter the flurry of questions, the answer that always came was "love." Love for humanity. Love for the families torn apart by racial violence. Love for the beauty I see in each culture that should be praised instead of persecuted. Love for the light of unity connecting all beings as one.

Sensing the love I felt the moment needed, I thought of Dr. Martin Luther King, Jr.'s beautifully loving words. I posted a meme of one of his statements that read, "Darkness cannot drive out darkness; only light can do that. Hate cannot drive out hate; only love can do that." I felt that if there was ever a point in history for Dr. King's words to gather and uplift people, it was this one.

With so much repressed pain and anger erupting in the ethers of the collective, a vocal few took exception to my post. They assumed I was criticizing the protests, as if it was not spiritual to step outside of our comfort zone and take to the streets. This couldn't have been further from the truth. I was merely sharing the words that provided me inspiration during such a dark hour of grief and despair.

Someone commented: "We are not just going to get over it because it makes your white privilege uncomfortable." That broke my heart. My inner freedom fighter was gutted. No one said anything about the words coming from MLK, despite the fact that the meme contained his name and picture. It was a moment when my image was reduced to a generalization of racial divide, when a select few used me as the best place for their projections to land.

I had to ask myself, *Were these really projections? What if I'm the one who doesn't actually get it? What if I'm so blinded by privilege, statements that I think are helpful might be patronizing to others with differing experiences? Maybe I'm missing something.* For the first time in my life, I called into question my deepest ethical values. I wasn't even sure whether I really stood for the equality I had always defended.

I sat on my couch like a warrior collapsed on his sword, watching groups scream, "Black lives matter!" while others yelled hurtful dismissive words of intolerance: "All lives matter!" Deep down, I knew who I was and exactly what I stood for. Yet, not even the words of MLK could soothe the raging fire of anger permeating all corners of the globe.

During this time, I noticed many people come together in support of greater community outreach and more extensive neighborhood program funding. But I also saw a collective unconsciousness use this moment to instigate violence, loot storefronts, and burn down communities as if these acts were a justification that had waited for the perfect time to erupt within people hungry for something to destroy.

Only an hour had passed since I'd posted the MLK meme, and the mixture of support and criticism continued to build. Out of a place of pain and confusion and not knowing how to stand in the face of this type of discord, I deleted it. This was a moment when the ever-bearing fruit of love seemed so unlikely out of season. Then I got lumped into categories such as "Just another spiritual teacher hiding behind their white privilege." Such hurtful comments had nothing to do with my standpoint, my support for equality; nor did it actually matter to the profound change brewing in me.

At first I thought, *This is what others must have experienced*. But then, an even deeper wisdom began shining through. It said, *No. This is not what other races or minorities experience. This is a tiny sliver of what life is like when you walk even for a moment in the shoes of the oppressed. You're being ridiculed on social media for a few minutes. You've never felt your life threatened, had a loved one killed, or been roughed up by a police officer just because your race matches a profile. Your experience isn't like what other races feel or have lived through.*

This is you getting an empathic glimpse into a fraction of the pain that has been buried under society's skin for generations . . . from people shipped from their homeland to live as servants to white families and aristocrats to kids being separated from their parents at the border and the drastic ways police enforcement differs from zip code to zip code. Meanwhile, you have the time, space, and capacity to fathom that pain without worrying about where your next meal will come from or when bullets will spray through your living room window.

As these thoughts penetrated my soul, I broke down in a puddle of tears, as a surprising truth revealed itself: being an empath provided me a keen awareness of other people's feelings, but only from my point of view—like an objective witness who could feel each person's emotions but never from their unique vantage point of lived experiences. As this truth deepened, I began to see the subtle mask I'd hidden behind, imagining that my empathic abilities gave me a clue about what life was really like for people who were racially oppressed. *What a socially acceptable form of arrogance*, I thought. Even though it was neither intentional nor malicious, I had believed that by tuning in from the standpoint of my culture's safe haven, I would be able to encapsulate another person's struggles. I now realized that I couldn't.

This shift fundamentally transformed my response of, *I understand*, to *Please help me better understand what I've never faced and may never encounter*. This was the deepest compassion I had ever felt, and it came from admitting to myself with brutal honesty what I can't know from my own history of experiences. The realization expanded to include discrimination based on gender and sexual orientation, to even what life was like for someone who had escaped a war-torn country. I sat in my living room, sobbing and shaking while admitting to myself, *I will never know the pain of a woman losing the child she was birthing. I will never know the unfairness of working twice as hard for half as much. I will never know the confusion of being born in what feels like the wrong body or the intensity of fearing that my inner truth could cost me a place in my family. I will never know the uncertainty of wondering if a friend who's absent from school was hurt or killed in the latest bomb attack.*

With the Universe as my witness, I confessed everything I thought I understood on a visceral level and admitted to myself, *No matter how I try to rationalize reality by thinking I understand, the heartbreaking truth is I don't. All I can do is be the best example of my race, gender, and individuality to give others an opportunity to find safety in the presence of human symbols that have translated into oppression, injustice, bigotry, persecution, and suffering. May I be a space that hears the testimony of others, not filtered through cultural convenience or socialized generalization but from a depth of understanding my lack of direct experiences. In that way, I hope to give others a platform to be seen, heard, and healed on a more profound level.*

As someone who had never been regularly subjected to unfair treatment, it was my right, honor, and privilege to listen, hold the despair of other people's pain, and offer a shoulder for them to cry on as I sobbed on theirs. No longer was "I understand" a part of my vocabulary. While others perpetuated racial divide with statements like "Get over it" or "All lives matter," I for one, would never get over this realization or let it float away out of the convenience of memory.

Energetically exhausted and emotionally battered, I'd never felt more alive than I did on that fateful day.

The Attribute of Patience

While your ego may think it can fathom the experience of others based on perceptions of similarities and differences, you will never truly comprehend the gravity of someone's living testimony by virtue of comparison. You will only know the direct visceral nature of each moment by the space you allow for others to be heard and received. While it can be quite subtle to distinguish between listening to your understanding of another person's journey and allowing them to relive harrowing moments in your presence, patience is often the key.

As the next attribute in the space-holding process, patience is the time you spend showing genuine interest toward another person's reality. The more you believe you wholeheartedly understand the complexities of people existing outside yourself, the more you may slide into impatience when they share more or go on longer than your ego can handle. Equally so, the more aware you are that you can't truly comprehend someone's firsthand account without walking lifetimes in their shoes, the more you can learn from all they are meant to share.

Through the attribute of patience, you'll understand why other people see you differently than you may view yourself. While you have had many years to know your unique qualities, for another, you may exist solely as a symbol of the suffering they have endured. Patience also helps you give others the space to be exactly where they are in their journey, since so many people are far too steeped in the intensity of their own pain to know how you would prefer them to see or treat you. With patience as your guide, the more honest you are about how little people have in common with each other, the more likely you will be to learn from the subjectivity of someone's sharing and even create space for them to learn from you.

In the old spiritual paradigm, the interconnection of oneness was a bond created from an awareness of similarity. From this surface level of interaction, the more you and I found how much we had in common, the safer we would feel and the less threatening it would be for us to connect. While this may be how strangers turn into friends, neighbors, coworkers, and even life partners, the deeper connection of oneness occurs when we appreciate the incredible differences that exist among all of us. While the ego interprets a lack of similarity as a threat rather than an opportunity, once you accept how little you and others have in common, a greater space of interest can be created for all to explore.

This reminds me of a twenty-eight-day trip I took to India. Whenever store owners approached me, they would ask, "What do you know about India?"

My reply would be, "I don't know anything about India. I'm just so excited to be here and learn."

My exuberance seemed infectious to those I met, as I was aware of being a visitor in a foreign country and was not trying to impose my culture on theirs. Even if I had learned a few things about India, it would have just been my understanding of their way of life as perceived through my cultural lens. To the best of my ability, I wanted to experience this country like those who lived there. While many people from the tour were confused and angered by a culture so opposite to their own, I was able to remain open, excited, and inspired by all the differences between me and the people living in this majestic foreign land.

While the old spiritual paradigm equates oneness with sameness, it creates a tendency in which you are likely to be completely open only around those of like mind and similar nuances of experience. In the new spiritual paradigm, oneness is not about looking, talking, or acting like any other person. It's a direct view into the infinite tapestry of diversity, where beings emanating from one eternal source experience the endless ways spirit expresses itself through the uniqueness of all.

When you're guided by the attribute of patience, you're no longer in a hurry to find common ground or rush someone through their experience by claiming to understand it. In truth, you only know yourself: the way you think and interpret, the categories you create, and how you compare and contrast your perceptions of others based on your singular history of choices, conditioning, and experiences.

This is why patience is the guiding light of compassion. The more you admit to only truly knowing your view of life, no matter how empathic or psychically gifted you may be, the more open you can be to learning how different life is for others, even when they're standing next to you in the same moment in time.

What Could Possibly Go Wrong?

When you embody patience, you experience a high level of emotional endurance that conveys the depth of your presence. Equally so, working through varying degrees of impatience helps you break through to new horizons of tolerance, faithfulness, and acceptance. While it's always useful to view even the most inconsequential moments as opportunities to strengthen your patience, when pushed too far, your ego might lash out or shut down. If this occurs, it is important to shift the space you are holding for others toward taking time for yourself. When your ego's most reactive behaviors—shifts from openness to irritation, an inability to listen or be interested in other people's sharing, or even the yearning to be somewhere else—arise, it's a signal that you may be offering more energy to others than you are able to provide for your own emotional needs. The tendency to overlook how little you have to give highlights what could possibly go wrong on the journey of ever-growing patience.

In order for you to cultivate patience, you must wholeheartedly respect the signs of overgiving that moments of impatience convey. It requires a keen level of discernment to recognize which moments can be pushed beyond the threshold of your comfort zone and when to end engagements in support of your own self-care. The more skillful you become at holding greater space for yourself, the better you'll be at noticing the defense mechanisms of ego as reminders calling you inward for greater rejuvenation.

Contrary to one of the ego's most popular assumptions, this doesn't mean you must immediately end an interaction once impatience arises. You may just need to excuse yourself from a lunch meeting or the dinner table to get some fresh air. After a few moments of breathing, you may notice that you've been able to release the cluster of emotions that were triggered. If your sense of impatience returns, it may be an indication that you have reached a point of exhaustion with nothing left to offer others from within a state of depletion. This becomes evident as increasing intolerance for the differences in others.

From a space-holding perspective, how can anyone be best served if you're not at your best? How can anyone benefit if you're trying to give from a state of deficiency? From this greater awareness, you will become an incredible space holder for yourself, no longer caught in tendencies of overgiving as impatience helps you acknowledge irritability, depletion, and exhaustion as the ways your inner child is begging for a nap.

Setting an Intention for Patience

To embrace the true meaning of oneness and hold a space of patience for yourself and others, please repeat the following words out loud:

I intend to hold space through the attribute of patience
for myself and others as the grace of embodied presence.
I allow patience to be offered from a space of genuine

interest, where I am able to feel greater connections with others when allowing them to be sovereign, unique expressions of spirit unlike the shape, form, and way I have come to be. I recognize the attribute of patience as a gift I am free to share, as it helps me recognize the diversity of life as the space through which intimacy and equality grow. From this space, I allow the evolution of ego, like an innocent child growing within me, to integrate and mature so I may cultivate a greater capacity of patience for those I meet.

In knowing it is so, I allow the attribute of patience to inspire the uniqueness of all, no matter how it's received, overlooked, or denied, or whether I agree with the viewpoints of any personal sharing. If and when this hurts my feelings, triggers memories of past traumas, makes me more distrusting of others, causes me to shut down in rejection or lash out in resentment, or instigates palpable signs of exhaustion, I allow myself the sacred space to be with my feelings and offer the gift of patience to any exhausted part of me. Whether given to myself or another person or as an active blessing to humanity, I welcome the attribute of patience to widen the parameters of my perception, acknowledging through the eyes of oneness how differently we all grow together. And so it is.

The Supportive Statement of Patience

"We Are in No Rush—Please Take Your Time"

Through the attribute of patience, you embrace someone's journey from their viewpoint and not just from feedback filtered through your perceptions. This allows others the space to openly share what they feel safe enough to divulge. This is why the supportive statement of patience is "We are in no rush—please take your time." Assuming you have the time to give, why shouldn't others know they are free to slow down and savor each feeling or concern?

While others' emotional sharing may occur more slowly than yours, through the attribute of patience, your ability to be present with their process creates equal opportunities to deepen your relationship with your own feelings as uniquely depicted in another person's life. Even when moving throughout your day, your ability to gently remind yourself, *We are in no rush—please take your time*, allows you to complete the most menial tasks with greater ease and attention to detail. Through the attribute of patience, the less personally you interpret other people's behavior, the fewer expectations you'll project and the less likely you'll be to define fulfillment by needing life to go in one way instead of another.

When "We are in no rush—please take your time" becomes the speed your life is lived, you will meet each uncertainty with more openness and excitement instead of perpetual irritation.

Patience in Action

Through the attribute of patience, you are able to honor the individual journeys of all people as unique expressions of divinity in human form.

Perhaps you are interacting with someone who has been marginalized for so long, they instinctively associate your gender, sexual orientation, culture, religion, or skin color with past abuses of power. Instead of feeling judged or unfairly lumped into a category, what if you saw this interaction as an opportunity to embody patience and represent your race, gender, sexual orientation, culture, religion, or personality in such a way that it offers corrective experiences in support of greater healing?

Maybe an endless list of tasks is not really the Universe treating you like an overworked assistant but a means through which slowing down and taking your time can instill a greater capacity of patience in you. What if people who are impatient with you exist in your life to help you practice being more patient with them? Perhaps beyond the superstitious beliefs of ego, other people's unprocessed pain doesn't actually lower your energetic vibration but merely reflects your own exhaustion, which urges you to make more time for personal renewal. Maybe the constant need to change jobs, shift careers, swap out romantic partners, move locations, or reinvent yourself is only a necessity for the most impatient aspects of self.

What if nothing in your life needs to change other than the space you hold in order to discover the true fulfillment that you seek?

Patience as a Daily Practice

To bring the attribute of patience to the forefront of your awareness, try one or all of these daily practices:

- To help develop greater patience, allow mindfulness to lead the way when accomplishing each daily task. Whether it's brushing your teeth more deliberately, chewing carefully and savoring the tastes and textures of each meal, or even making your bed each morning, may the simplest tasks assist you in finding greater meaning simply by helping you become more connected to what you're doing.

- During moments of annoyance, remember to take mini breathing breaks. When exhaustion is apparent, dare to give yourself the right to rest, despite the demands or insistence of others.

- Aspire to meet each person as a soul in physical form, embracing their race, gender, sexual orientation, personal preferences, and even their emotional triggers as differences to honor within the oneness of life. May you meet each person openly, as if for the very first time to offer them the time, space, and capacity to be a better version of themselves than ever before. Whether or not it helps them show up differently, may you always respect the beauty of diversity by not defining others in any particular way.

CHAPTER 7

Boundaries Are an Act of Self-Love

s an empathic being, it's natural to overgive due to how deeply you sense the feelings of others and how much you wish for the world to be happy. Because empaths are emotionally hardwired healers mirroring and transmuting the traumas buried in others, their feelings can be intense while striving to remain open with this incredible gift to share. Although an emotionally sensitive person can help others transform perceptions of vulnerability from a sense of insecurity or weakness into a wellspring of spiritual power, empaths are also on their own journey of evolution. It is important for them to establish personal boundaries, since it is their common subconscious motivation to help others feel good, so they themselves can have a better experience.

No matter how subtly or dramatically you have experienced emotional sensitivities, the tendency to overgive stems from not knowing how to distinguish your feelings from the sensations of others. This was certainly my dilemma, even though I wasn't able to name or understand it until well into adulthood. I remember sensing surges of emotions when interacting with other kids. I would often misinterpret these feelings as their opinion of me. This led me to create a false, although compelling belief suggesting, *No one likes me. Everyone hates me. And until I can experience their happiness, I don't feel accepted by them.*

It's humbling to recognize how many years one can maintain such false beliefs without realizing how exhausting it is to carry them around. Because I assumed I was only accepted when other people were happy, it became my unapologetic role in childhood to cheer everyone up. As a young empath, I took on each emotion that I sensed in others as a mask of low self-esteem that I wore while searching for validation outside myself. After many years of playing out this pattern, I would come to see that such a mask of low self-esteem seemed nearly impenetrable, no matter how often or how much anyone approved of me.

This is why people who have difficulty distinguishing their feelings from the experiences of others tend to seek refuge in ego. While my inner child could recite a long, painful list of people I served with dedication only to have them discard me when they were done with me, as an adult, I developed a more supportive perspective around this pattern. Yes, I overgave in nearly every relationship I had. Yes, others offered approval to the best of their ability. Yes, many meaningful relationships vanished without explanation. Yes, I felt like everyone's healer in a world with very few reliable companions. And yes, it can be quite isolating when you've learned to "rescue" others as a way of having some semblance of connection, no matter how fleeting or one-sided the relationship might be.

While it took years to come out from behind the disappointment, heartbreak, and resentment I felt toward others, over time, I began to see the dynamic of relationships from a much higher level. The actions I once interpreted as rejection or abandonment actually gave me extraordinary periods of alone time. This helped me get to know the visceral nature of my own experiences without confusing them with the feelings of others.

Inevitably, the more time I spent getting to know myself, the easier it became for me to separate my emotions from other people's reactions. It was as if my feelings had a specific frequency of sensation, much like the fragrance I noticed when walking down the detergent aisle in the grocery store. When around others whose emotions gave off a different quality, if I couldn't smell the sweet scent of detergent, I knew the emotions weren't mine to explore and must be experiences belonging to people strolling other aisles in the grocery store of life.

This awareness became my first experience of boundaries. It also gave me tremendous relief from the constant need to seek approval by trying to cheer everyone up. It helped me ground and remain centered in the uniqueness of my individual perception, as a way of acknowledging and honoring the differing experiences other people had the right to have. From these encounters, I have come to understand the importance of space, even celebrating boundaries as an act of self-love. With the time and maturity required to bring each mysterious clue together, I was able to sense how accepted I was, how worthy I am, and how whole I have always been through my connection with the Universe.

Perhaps this is not just my story but an epic saga you're living out too. With greater respect toward your sensitivities and the subjective experiences of others, may it spark the completion of your hero's redemption, ending the existential tragedy where nearly everyone feels great in your presence—except for you.

The Attribute of Respect

There is a certain definition of *respect* that truly highlights a central theme in holding space: "A due regard for the feelings, wishes, rights, or traditions of others." In order to show such regard, it is essential to honor an awareness and adherence to personal space, above and beyond any desire, preference, or expectation you may have. When boundaries are an act of self-love, the attribute of respect helps you find the inner worth to ask for and accept the space you or others need.

When I was a child, I didn't know that personal space existed. I'd spend my alone time playing video games or exploring my imagination. These activities helped me hide from the unworthiness of feeling invisible to the world around me. At that time, I believed the existence of someone's personal boundary was a rude, selfish, and offensive form of rejection. Even if I could step back in time and say to my younger self, "Hey there, buddy. It's me from the future. I traveled back in time to give you some advice. You know those people who need their own space that you interpret as selfish, rude, and offensive? Well, they're actually just protecting their energy, as is their sovereign right and privilege. Boundaries are more about their needs than about you. Just so you know."

Without missing a beat, I'm sure my younger self would have replied, "Why do they need to protect their energy? Are they saying I'm gross?" With time and greater maturity came the realization that relationships blossom from a fertile ground of mutual respect—a respect that allows everyone the right to their own decisions, perceptions, and process, no matter how much I want to engage and connect during moments when space would benefit everyone. When leading with respect, it's not just how attentive you are in someone's presence but how willing you are to offer space for experiences that may not include your involvement. It is important to know that your ego will never understand this partirular point since it often believes, *Why would anyone need space from me? Have you met me? I'm fantastic! I have so much to give and share.*

This is where codependency gets confused with loyalty, over-giving masquerades as attentiveness, and personal boundaries are interpreted as moments of rejection. The solution to this degree of ego involvement is the same as when empathic sensitivities are resolved: the space you establish to get to know yourself on deeper levels will help you make peace with and even enjoy the benefits of personal boundaries. Through the attribute of respect, you honor your physical body as your vessel of evolution that requires rest in order to recharge. Just like a car that hasn't been properly fueled, if there isn't enough gas in the tank, you can't take the journey you have envisioned.

The ego's fight against creating boundaries is much like the temperament of a child who is too bored in silence and stillness to give themselves the rest they truly need. Simply put, you will never offend people who really love you with requests of personal space. On the other hand, those who only interpret this need as a rejection haven't yet learned how to love authentically. Also, those who don't know how to love authentically haven't discovered their own empathic nature. This prevents them from having an awareness of how much energy an empath like you needs to function in daily life as a living vessel of healing moving through space and time. Others may think that you're just doing a series of chores or menial tasks. Yet, when experienced from inside the sensory perception of an energetically attuned and emotionally sensitive person, a few simple errands can be quite exhausting given the energy they transmit.

With the attribute of respect as your guide, you'll create and maintain boundaries as an act of self-love without needing to debate their necessity with others, prove your needs, or explain yourself in any way. To love yourself is to respect yourself. To respect yourself is to love giving yourself all that you need to be at your best. To love others is to respect their process as much as you honor your own. To respect others is to love seeing that their needs are met, whether in your presence or your absence.

Such a definitive connection between respect, love, and the importance of proper boundaries celebrates the true fulfillment of intimacy. Through the attribute of respect, you create a sustainably loving connection in which two hearts unite in the mutual desire to support the well-being and fulfillment of each other.

Through the attribute of respect, may your most loving intentions and excitement to connect be grounded and balanced by the appropriate amount of space, which may differ for each person and circumstance. May any tendency of taking personally the boundaries other people establish be acknowledged as a gift you are able to provide, perhaps in a way you least expect or desire. May the value of respect be of equal importance to the desire to love and be loved. May you take the time to acknowledge how the needs of one could only be of mutual evolutionary benefit for all involved.

What Could Possibly Go Wrong?

While the value of respect is never a problem, your dilemma often hinges on how someone misinterprets and disrespects the need for personal space. In fact, it's common for people to misconstrue the gift of space as a punishment or "time out," motivating their ego to figure out how to be a better accepted and more appealing version of themselves. This tactic overlooks the true need for space as a golden opportunity to recharge before further engagement.

Even when someone accuses you of hurting them in response to the space you have asked for, their accusation doesn't necessarily mean that you've done anyone harm. This is often an unfamiliar way for empaths to think, but just because someone may interpret your needs as a form of rejection doesn't mean you should overlook the space you need, even if you live your life afraid of hurting others.

One of the reasons that the request for personal space can feel like rejection is due to a parent's modeled behavior of codependency that can easily be confused with the virtue of dedication. When this occurs, children witness a parent giving all the energy they have without leaving anything for themselves. Whether modeled by a parent, another family's dynamic, or even a schoolteacher, when tendencies to overgive, overpromise, and overdeliver occur in the name of unconditional love—without showing equal respect to the person constantly giving—codependency becomes confused with dedication. A person conditioned in this way ends up feeling dismissed when someone around them needs their space. This causes their ego to identify itself as a problem in the life of the person who needs distance for their own recharging. The ego often wonders how to get back in their good graces, to be less of a problem and more of a benefit to the one they interpret as having judged, rejected, or abandoned them.

When the pattern of overgiving is active, it is common to feel resentful, unseen, or undervalued if you're engaged with someone who doesn't respond to your actions with the same intensity that you display. This is often why a person stuck in the pattern of codependency works so hard to keep others happy, since their sense of safety, acceptance, and normalcy lives and dies based on the temperament of the people they are afraid of being separated from.

Especially when someone requests a need for space, any reaction of cruelty, harassment, or shaming will distinguish patterns of obsession from true love. In love, you cultivate connections in the time you spend together and strengthen them during moments spent faithfully apart. But if someone's insecurities, unfounded jealousy, or short-temperedness seem to flare whenever you implement boundaries, this is often a sign of them attempting to love through the unconscious tendency of obsession. When obsession occurs, you may feel more like an object that person possesses and controls than a person being valued and respected in true intimate partnership.

Through the attribute of respect, you can care for your own needs from a space of renewed empowerment, without needing to align with someone else's beliefs about how you should spend your time and energy.

Setting an Intention for Respect

To unravel codependency and hold a space of respect for yourself and others, please repeat the following words out loud:

I intend to hold space through the attribute of respect for myself and others from a space of assertive clarity. I allow respect to be offered from such a depth of discernment, where I am able to notice the difference between unconditional love and obsession by how I or others respond to the implementation of personal boundaries. Because personal boundaries are not always in response to other people's behavior, but what I require in order to be open and share without overgiving, I honor how precisely the necessity of boundaries deepens my practice of self-love, while also showing me who is truly capable of loving me from an aligned, conscious standpoint. By embracing the gift of space as a way of resolving any degree of empathic confusion, I allow all patterns of codependency to be cleared out of my energy field, returned to the Source of its origin, transmuted completely, and healed to completion now.

In knowing it is so, I allow the attribute of respect to call forward the highest emotional maturity in all, no matter how it's received, overlooked, or denied, or whether I agree with the viewpoints of any personal sharing. If and when this hurts my feelings, triggers memories of past traumas, makes me more distrusting of others, causes me to shut down in rejection or lash out in resentment, or instigates palpable signs of exhaustion, I allow myself the sacred space to be with my feelings and offer the gift of respect to any disgruntled part of me. Whether given to myself or another person or as an active blessing to humanity, I allow the attribute of respect to help me communicate my personal needs without requiring the permission of others, in order to do what is right for me. And so it is.

The Supportive Statement of Respect

"I Wish I Could Give More, but My Time Has Come"

In an attempt to be clear in your boundary-making, a supportive sentence such as "I wish I could give more, but my time has come" allows you to confirm how honorably you are communicating your need for space. While someone can feel hurt in response to disappointment, your ability to inform them that you must be fully present with your own personal needs helps you empathize with the pain stirring in them without making their issue a problem for you to fix.

As a metaphor, imagine sitting in the backseat during an Uber ride. Suddenly, the car stops a few blocks before reaching your destination. The driver turns to you and says, "As much as I'd love to complete your trip, I've run out of gas. I regret to inform you that our trip will end here."

Just as this driver would love to finish the journey with you, if only they had more fuel, each of us would love to be the exact versions of ourselves other people desire us to be. As the ongoing demands of life remind you of how little energy you have for anyone but yourself, you either choose self-care from a space of self-respect or cater to the insatiable whims of other people's obsessions. When you express, "I wish I could give more, but my time has come," you can then distinguish who has the capacity to occupy deeper places in your heart based on their depth of respect. Those who challenge your needs or disregard their existence are actually offering you the gift of greater clarity. It helps you see who wants to be part of your life solely for the benefit it provides them.

As you recognize this distinction, people who fight against the space you need confirm just how important boundaries are.

Equally so, these statements are important to voice because, just as common as it can be to feel rejected by others' boundaries, it is equally natural to take space for yourself without openly communicating your needs to others. Since empaths often fear the wrath of disapproval, we often attend to our own needs in secrecy, which can come off as being standoffish, avoidant, and disconnected to a person who has no idea of what we need and may be afraid to convey.

Through the supportive statement "I wish I could give more, but my time has come," you are learning to live from an unconditionally loving space, while maintaining a level of maturity that allows honest communication to be the foundation for any evolving connection.

In the beginning, such a statement can feel as if you're crushing someone's dreams or are about to be rejected by not measuring up to their standards. But, the more often you articulate, "I wish I could give more, but my time has come," the less likely you'll be to apologize for your own needs. Even when it seems as if you are the only one holding such an honorable perspective throughout your life, it's your ability to stand tall in the face of loneliness that will open greater space for more respectful people to enter your reality.

Respect in Action

Through the attribute of respect, by allowing your own needs to be honored, you no longer confuse love with obsession or connect through overgiving.

Perhaps you are running late at the very moment a friend has important news to share. You keep telling your friend, "I want to hear all about this, but I really don't have time right now." But they continue to engage and bargain for more of what you don't have. Will you allow yourself to be late? Will you see this person as the Universe testing how kind you are? Or will you appreciate this interaction as the chance to gently let them know that you're unable to give them what they want right now?

Maybe your healing journey, the demands of your work life, or even household dynamics with your partner and kids have left you feeling exhausted and overwhelmed. As the holidays roll around, you dread family members who can't see beyond their idealized image of the holidays to support your need for alone time. Will you give yourself the space you need while allowing them to see you as the character they project onto you? Or will you disrespect yourself by choosing to meet the expectations of unconscious family dynamics?

What if you're in the early stages of dating a person, and you ask what they do to nourish themselves when they're alone? If they haven't created opportunities to be alone or don't see the importance of alone time, it may confirm that even though they may appear to have the best intentions, they might still be relating from a space of obsession. While you can't use one question to place someone in a box, the lack of spaciousness in someone else's life may foreshadow the equal lack of space you may feel if you choose to engage further.

Perhaps you are the one fearing rejection or abandonment by not knowing how to respect someone else's boundaries. If this is the case, can their need for space become an opportunity to hold loving space for yourself?

Maybe, despite your best attempts to be present, a work commitment or snafu at home prevented you from attending your child's performance or championship game. What if no matter how many apologies you offer, your child still holds this against you? Can you use the importance of boundaries to respect the space they need to process their grief, knowing a parent's role is to love unconditionally, no matter how inconsistent a child's love may feel?

Respect as a Daily Practice

To bring the attribute of respect to the forefront of your awareness, try one or all of these daily practices:

- Begin to use the supportive statements from this and previous chapters, to minimize how often you say, "I'm sorry." Since people frequently use this expression when they don't know what else to say, may the consciousness communicated in each supportive statement help you be more direct and specific. While you can convey empathy toward others' misfortunes with "I'm sorry," by replacing it with more supportive words, such as "I wish I could give more, but my time has come," you hold space for the clear communication of your choices without allowing the other person's experience to outweigh the importance of yours.

- As a visualization, imagine traveling back in time to meet with, console, and love the younger parts of yourself that are still caught in the past. As you intuitively select an age or choose one based on your wounds, imagine meeting with your younger parts and even watching as they dissolve into the body of your adult self. If you're unsure which version of your younger self to select, you can always ask your heart which parts need to be returned to safety through the love only you can provide.

- If you find yourself obsessing about a past lover, other people's hurtful actions, or conspiracy theories you're driven to figure out by scouring the internet, dare to engage in more productive acts of self-love to replace lingering habits of obsession. Whether it's taking a breathing break, saying "I love you" to your heart, getting some fresh air, or even engaging in exercise, every empowered choice helps break up the stagnant energy of compulsive patterning. Each time you exchange compulsion for choices of self-empowerment, you are remembering how your spectrum of choices determines the quality of your experiences.

CHAPTER 8

Gratitude Is
Always Appropriate

From a very early age, the existence of God has always intrigued me. While the household I was raised in was not
devoutly religious, God was always the name my family
attributed to the magic and miracles of Source energy. Whether you resonate with terms like *the Universe, light, consciousness,
truth, oneness, spirit, divinity*, or even just *the One*, perhaps you
too have been spellbound by the magnificent beauty and unthinkable perfection that can sneak into your awareness at the
most unexpected times. Even as a child, the more I opened to
my growing existential curiosity, the more such a divine presence
entered my experience.

In support of this resonance I felt toward divinity, my parents had taught me that God dwelled in everything and was
a loving, wise, merciful presence that only wanted the best

for me. This was a soothing message and was just the spark I needed to begin my inner journey.

I had also started going to Sunday school around the age of eleven in preparation for my Bar Mitzvah. There, spontaneous "knowings" began dropping in more regularly. I would hear biblical tales of a wrathful God, and I just sensed within the core of my being how "man-made" that felt. Without understanding why or how, I intrinsically could discern the difference between an idea of God and the direct truth of divinity itself. I didn't even realize that I knew this at the time, it was just an obvious distinction between "here is what man created God to be to keep people in check" and the ineffable, ever-present light of spirit.

Some of my friends grew up dreaming to be the next Michael Jordan. Others yearned to follow in their parents' footsteps by joining law enforcement. For me, the passion was inward. I wanted to commune with Source on the deepest level in a way that only made natural sense to the instincts within me. I wanted to have a front row seat to witness the immaculate glory of divinity in action while aspiring to be the clearest reflection of holy presence and serve the highest will of that which had called me into being.

One pivotal moment of sensing such divine holiness occurred when I was in the fifth grade. It was one of those winter afternoons when kids attended a school assembly to hear the choir sing holiday songs. You had your usual playlist of Christmas jingles with a few Hanukah melodies sprinkled in. But as the choir began to sing, "Do You Hear What I Hear?" I felt an eruption of energy building within me. All I could think of was, *I need to find somewhere to let this out. If not, I'm going to really embarrass myself.*

I ran out of the auditorium and made it halfway across the schoolyard, where I emitted the most guttural shriek and began sobbing uncontrollably. I wasn't in pain, upset, hurt, or angry. I was somehow tapping into the pure reverence of spirit coming to life within the core of my being. It was like something deep inside me had become unleashed. I had no clue what was happening, but I knew I was safe and secure in the presence of an invisible loving force.

While I would have profound glimpses of this truth throughout childhood and adolescence, my growing awareness began ramping up more frequently during my early adulthood. As it blossomed, I was particularly intrigued by the power and expression of gratitude. I had initially discovered subtle forms of gratitude in middle school, primarily as a defense mechanism against bullying. A group of kids would approach me to mock my height. I remember them saying, "Dude! You're short."

In response, something inside inspired me to say, "I am. Thanks for noticing." They would look at me as if I'd made the dumbest comeback in history and then storm off. Apparently, making fun of me wasn't entertaining for them since I hadn't given them the opposition they craved.

As I matured, gratitude would resurface in response to other people's judgments. I would genuinely think, *Thank you for taking the time to notice me as a part of your life, no matter how you choose to see me.* Each time I chose to be grateful, I experienced a rather surprising, intoxicating bliss. Despite the hurtful words coming my way, I felt held, safe, and secure just like I did on that sacred wintery day in the fifth grade.

As this practice continued to evolve during my young adulthood, my childhood love of video games inspired me to think about gratitude creatively. Each time I offered gratitude to anything, I would imagine adding more points to my vibrational score. As I began seeing life through the eyes of gratitude, it became obvious to me that each interaction, outcome, and circumstance was a gift created to inspire my highest and greatest good—even when it was packaged in a form that was confusing, overwhelming, or frustrating to encounter.

The more I led with gratitude, the more settled I felt in my body, the more peace I sensed throughout the world, and the more connected I felt to others—no matter our differences in opinion or however they chose to see me. It became quite liberating to realize how I didn't need to control anyone's viewpoints or choices when I had access to the bliss that gratitude offers. It still didn't make me best friends with those fed by ridiculing others, but it shifted my perspective enough to see the subjective and often unbearable nature of someone else's experience that I didn't have to interpret as a judgment or attack against me. Since the more appreciation I offered, the more steeped in spirit I felt myself to be, gratitude became a way for me to walk through life as an empath protected by the presence of light depending upon how open, unguarded, and grateful I allowed myself to be. It was as if I held a silent agreement to welcome each person as expressions of Source, no matter how they had subconsciously agreed to present themselves or view me in return.

You'd think this would have made me a target for greater attacks and criticism. Yet, the opposite seemed to occur.

The Attribute of Appreciation

As your most inherent form of energetic and emotional protection, the attribute of appreciation requires no safe haven from other people's pain. As you shift from only appreciating what people do for you (or even withholding appreciation when you don't like their choices) to celebrating who human beings are underneath it all, you take a deeper dive into your own divinity from the inside out.

There are many in today's culture who get distracted from the importance of appreciation with social media–based labels such as *like* or *dislike*. These judgments are categories you place people in that determine, for better or for worse, how you treat them. The ego lives by its own self-serving version of personal values. It believes anything it *likes* should get your best qualities of character (your love, praise, and affection), while everything it *dislikes* is worthy of a cold shoulder, being ghosted, or your most defensive and often hurtful reactions. Because the ego is initially fueled by the conditioning of unresolved pain within you, it operates from this level of reactivity, as if anything it dislikes should be blamed for taking up space and preventing more of what it wants or likes from entering reality.

While your true ethics urge you to treat others the way you would like to be treated, the ego mainly responds to people judgmentally. When your ego dislikes, it can imagine it has been wronged, especially when someone behaves differently from how you usually view them. This can trigger the trauma response of fear in you. Even when you're around a stranger who acts out in ways you may not expect or enjoy witnessing, it is natural for the ego to shut down as a primal form of protection against the threat of the unknown. Perhaps this may help you see the ego from a more compassionate standpoint as the way human beings behave when run by the survival mode of fear.

Whether it is in how you relate to yourself or are treated by others, if you feel like a commodity that rises and falls in popularity within the ego's volatile stock market, the attribute of appreciation liberates you from this exhausting cycle of judgment. Since you can mercifully view the ego as the way you react when you are run by fear, it becomes more obvious that you are only capable of judging the things you are afraid of. But through the attribute of appreciation, you have no one to impress, absolutely nothing to prove, and no expectations to tiptoe around. Best of all, you no longer take so personally how often anyone shifts from like to dislike. Even when the judgments keep coming your way, it only reveals the existence of fear in those who do the judging.

Especially when holding space for yourself, by appreciating the fear-based reactive mechanism of ego as how your most hurtful parts attempt to protect themselves from the threat of loss or return of pain, you are able to listen deeply, honor authentically, and value how much more of your divinity shines through when you meet yourself in a heart-centered way. The more you culti-vate a loving relationship with your most fearful and judgmental parts, the less often you will imagine your negative self-talk as accurate and the more likely you will be to clearly see how those parts beg for the attention they don't know how to ask for or feel worthy enough to receive.

While the ego may try to personify itself as your fear-based protector, it is you who serves the role of being its liberator by how lovingly you engage with it. The more you interact from a space-holding perspective, the easier it will become for you to relate to others who still operate out of judgment and fear. Ultimately, you teach your ego how to receive by giving from a consistently safe and loving space. As the ego senses safety over a period of time, it inevitably relinquishes control of imagining you as a fragile object in need of protecting. Eventually the rhythm of your kind approach helps the ego learn that it can trust you despite a fear of losing the control it only thinks it has.

Even though the ego's control is only a belief, if you attempt to correct it, it will likely shut down in response to feeling mocked, attacked, or judged. The ego so often reacts this way when hearing something it doesn't want to consider because that threatens to unravel its world of denial. As a means of preserving the denial it misperceives as reality, the ego regularly checks its self-serving list of like and dislike, constantly moving people from one category to the other. This actually serves a higher purpose of exhausting the energy of fear. As the ego grows weary, it inevitably lets go of fear and denial, along with a world of like versus dislike it thought it had such a hold on.

This may help you empathize with judgments in yourself and others that reveal the active programming of fear. While holding space doesn't assume you must be everyone's best friend, you can soften inner rigidity when you become aware of the suffering and despair others endure, whether or not they have yet to recognize the survival mode they operate from. Equally so, just because each person's true nature is divine, it doesn't always mean that they have a rightful place in your life. You may not want to be close friends with someone who constantly puts you in the penalty box whenever they dislike your actions. At the same time, just because someone's behavior and awareness seem light-years away from more heart-centered action, it doesn't mean you are helping them evolve when their judgments toward you become retaliatory criticisms you send back to them in return.

No matter who you decide to spend time with, through the attribute of appreciation, you can bow in the presence of their divinity, even when they are dressed up as a cruel character helping you muster the courage to finally walk away.

This supports the realization of two fundamental truths: There's no reason to separate from your divinity by judging someone from whom you need space. And just because a person is helping you evolve, it doesn't mean you have to be an intimate part of their life.

What Could Possibly Go Wrong?

There is no true, long-lasting fulfillment when you operate from the fear-based mechanism of ego—when the judgments you have about others control the quality of your behavior. This is a fundamental truth the ego will never know simply because its conditioning can only assume, anticipate, desire, fear, fight, and judge. It has no capacity to self-reflect outside the domain of self-serving viewpoints. The ego was never designed to know that the feeling of discontent can act as an emotional interpretation of judging behavior. Your tendency to criticize often reflects how much unprocessed pain and unresolved fear you have yet to address. This doesn't excuse such behavior, nor does condemning it help resolve the pattern. It simply gives you a greater perspective, so as not to overly personalize the actions of others who unknowingly hide from a world of connection by dividing it into categories of like and dislike.

When you interact with people caught in a web of judgment, it's likely they won't interpret your appreciation as a "like," since their ego believes it must push back against the inconveniences of reality until what it judges changes to suit its expectations. You may lead with "I appreciate you" or "Thank you for this time together," only to be met with deep disdain when the other person's heart refuses to open up. From a space-holding perspective, you are simply offering the gifts of compassionate support through the evolving skill of conscious communication. When you lead with appreciation, nothing could possibly go wrong, unless you are as attached to specific outcomes as the other person's ego is identified with judgment.

You may have been dreaming of the day you and your partner would take a long-awaited romantic vacation only to experience their most reactive behavior due to stresses they can't seem to leave behind at the office. When their worries or frustrations are taken out on you—*someone they love*—you have every right to determine how often or intimately you wish to connect with them while appreciating the opportunity to act from a more discerning space of empowerment.

When you can appreciate the nature of divinity without being a servant to anyone's ego, you will be better able to ebb and flow with the mysterious journey of life you incarnated to master. As your self-worth skyrockets from the quality of space you hold, you will come to know the visceral meaning of the phrase "True happiness comes from within." When happiness is determined more by how you respond and less by circumstances that come and go, you will begin to taste the ecstasy of emotional freedom where you are able to be yourself, regardless of how others interpret your actions or define your existence.

Setting an Intention for Appreciation

To cultivate a more aligned connection with divinity, release tendencies of judgment and fear, and hold a space of appreciation for yourself and others, please repeat the following words out loud:

> I intend to hold space through the attribute of
> appreciation for myself and others from a more

interconnected space of emotional freedom. I allow appreciation to be offered in celebration of my true divine essence, fully alive in all, while respecting the journey any person takes to become aware of this eternal truth. While someone's behavior may not elicit my responses of like and may even be choices I dislike, I step beyond the facades of judgment and fear to offer the appreciation that can help a person evolve, no matter the condemnation I yearn to project on them. By embracing the attribute of appreciation as an entry point into a more aligned connection with divinity, I allow all tendencies of judgment and patterns of fear to be cleared from my energy field, returned to the Source of its origin, transmuted completely, and healed to completion now.

In knowing it is so, I allow the attribute of appreciation to call forward the beauty of emotional freedom in me, no matter how it's received, overlooked, or denied, or whether I agree with the viewpoints of any personal sharing. If and when this hurts my feelings, triggers memories of past traumas, makes me more distrusting of others, causes me to shut down in rejection or lash out in resentment, or instigates palpable signs of exhaustion, I allow myself the sacred space to be with my feelings and offer the gift of appreciation to any overlooked part of me. Whether given to myself or another person or as an active blessing to humanity, I welcome the attribute of appreciation to raise the bar of my personal values in celebration of the remembrance of divinity I meet in all. And so it is.

The Supportive Statement of Appreciation

"I Appreciate You Sharing This; I'm So Glad You Are Getting It Out Now"

Even while the divine exists within each human being, it's quite common to believe a most loving force of supernatural power couldn't possibly be present when misfortune occurs. This is why the attribute of appreciation is so essential in helping you remember and reconnect to the light of divinity within you. Instead of shutting down in survival mode during difficult times, you can become rooted in spirit. The more rooted in spirit you are, the more access you'll have to your most mature heart-centered attributes, such as those you are exploring in this book. While it's not your responsibility to instill this awareness in others, by leading with the attribute of appreciation, you will be so strongly rooted in your essence, you will find great fulfillment in allowing others the space to be exactly as they are without overlooking your own needs or allowing them to disrespect your boundaries.

This is why the supportive statement for the attribute of appreciation is "I appreciate you sharing this. I'm so glad you are getting it out now." By offering this sentiment, you remember how often other people's words and actions reflect where they are in their healing journey and are never a measure of your personal worth. Even when someone seems to dislike something about you, a statement such as this helps you honor the uniqueness of their self-expression without having to agree or disagree with or like or dislike their input in return.

When the attribute of appreciation helps you lean in instead of lashing out or shutting down, you can neutralize judgmental attacks by seeing them as gifts you choose to receive. In this way, you remember how the Universe only provides you with the versions of reality that help you evolve to your highest and greatest good. With the attribute of appreciation leading the way, you will come to see how many evolutionary gifts the Universe constantly provides. What if someone's criticism offers the gift of greater perspective? What if it helps you finally recognize the difference between their words and their actions, so you can get even clearer on where they stand in your life. Maybe you're the one who receives the unexpected gift of awareness in response to casting harsh judgments, whether onto yourself or others. What if offering yourself the supportive statement of appreciation in response to judging someone or something you dislike helps to liberate you from such patterns of attachment, while neutralizing the energy of judgment being projected out?

Even when you're holding space for yourself, you are best able to support the unraveling of your own inner defenses just by saying to your most pained or unlikeable parts, "I appreciate you sharing this. I'm so glad you are getting it out now." Such a statement allows you to hold the emotional barf bucket for everything you're ready to release.

From this space, each time you convey appreciation, the truth of divinity meets itself in physical form, helping to break individual and collective cycles of abuse, neglect, and trauma for the well-being of all.

Appreciation in Action

Since gratitude is always appropriate in offering the gift of divine recognition, it helps you remain rooted in spirit and aligned in truth as you move through each evolutionary milestone.

Perhaps you are in a family in which one can't express feelings without blame. While you are free to have a standoff with a relative's ego, you can always find a more compassionate way to navigate familial terrain by conveying gratitude from a space of authenticity. No matter how little there actually is to be grateful for, when you say, "I appreciate you sharing this. I'm so glad you are getting it out now," you offer greater support to your relative's experience without internalizing their projections, disputing their claims, or constantly needing to act in a way that puts you back in their good graces.

Maybe you are pushed to your personal limit by the cruelty, unfairness, and mistreatment you see in the world. While undoubtedly it's natural to dislike such atrocities, what if judging the actions you hate only creates more time and space for these egregious patterns to remain active in others? What if your appreciation isn't a form of like or spiritual bypassing but rather gratitude for the opportunity to witness the unconsciousness of the world that your most empowered actions and empathic energy field are helping to transform? What if you can appreciate the healing you offer to ensure that fewer people will be harmed just by facing life's most disturbing circumstances with openness instead of opposition?

Perhaps online groups and discussion forums rooted in gathering crowds to collectively dislike certain people, actions, or policies—even when they preach change for a greater good—are unconscious forms of mob mentality. Can you see how you only create "greater good" through the actions of greater goodness? Are you able to pierce the facade of justification that makes unconscious behavior seem reasonable when cast in the direction of collective "dislike"? Can you understand how neither side of like or dislike breaks the collective cycles of abuse until both are brought to justice and healed?

What if you spend time with your life partner who is engaged in an activity you don't particularly resonate with? While you could always find your own form of entertainment, why not use this as an opportunity to set aside judgment and appreciate what brings your partner so much joy? What if their ego is so engaged—as if they're actually a member of their favorite sports team—that you help them feel more accepted just by taking a brief moment to honor their pleasure?

Maybe regularly judging life on planet Earth as getting worse instead of better reminds you to go within and hold sacred space for yourself? What if instead of trying to appreciate the perceptions of life that feel so scary, irreversible, and overwhelming, you're able to acknowledge the most fearful parts of yourself that only know how to request loving attention by seeing through the lens of catastrophe.

Appreciation as a Daily Practice

To bring the attribute of appreciation to the forefront of your awareness, try one or all of these daily practices:

- Whenever judgment arises toward yourself or another, pause for a moment to find something worth appreciating about the person you're criticizing. Even if you feel locked inside the walls of your most negative viewpoint, simply take the time to say, *May the person I am judging be blessed with the gift of appreciation for the greater good of all.*

- In your journal, make a list of what you appreciate, adding ten to twenty entries each day without repeating. Take the time to scan your reality with excitement and joy in search of more examples to be grateful for, no matter how small they may be—your favorite outfit, your most prized possession, the ocean, your access to nature, and even the availability of your breath.

- To establish greater self-worth and inner safety, dare to approach someone you perceive as rude to let them know how much you appreciate them. Even if you don't welcome their behavior, what you offer becomes a moment of gratefulness sent from your essence to their divine nature. Only by stepping outside your comfort zone to give someone more than they provide can you dare to inspire a calmer environment for everyone's benefit.

CHAPTER 9

Facing "What Is" Can Be
Uncomfortable, and That's Okay

It's a true testament of faith to recognize the beneficial gifts throughout life's unexpectedly fierce and uncomfortable learning curve. Since most people carry within them wounds from their upbringing, it's quite possible that your current level of growth can remind you of a time when you felt punished. Through this association to the past, you may assume your discomfort is a sign of inner resistance or wrongdoing, as if you've somehow veered off your highest, destined path. But if the path you walk is destined, it's an endpoint you can't miss, stray from, or deny. As you cultivate greater understanding, you'll come to see how each moment prepares you for the next milestone of expansion with no punishments handed down or wrong turns taken, other than how you may perceive life when filtering it through the ego's most limiting beliefs.

The ego yearns to either maintain the control it only thinks it has or imagine ways to prove the control it will never truly find. Therefore, it cannot shake or reconcile the suffering that so often occurs when debating, bargaining, or negotiating with the inherent perfection of reality. While the ego insists, *Life would be so much better, if only I got my way!* the true growth of interconnection occurs when you can trust divinity completely, even when it's disguised as the shock and awe of unexpected change.

Having grown up afraid of nearly all conceivable things—including my own power—I constantly lived in a state of hypervigilance scanning each surrounding for any looming threat. As an adult, I could distill all my worries down to the fear of pain, which represented an invasive loss of control. But as my spiritual path progressed, I would use these old fears as profound moments of inquiry. I asked myself, *What is it about pain that makes it hurt so much?* I discovered an insightful difference in experience whenever, *This shouldn't be happening*, became brave moments of facing "what is."

This led to an incident that tested my newfound understanding with a surprising onrush of pain unlike anything I'd ever endured. It occurred about seven years ago when I was recovering from the flu. To boost my immune system, I used a product called grapefruit seed extract. The instructions on the small bottle said to add a few drops to water to dilute its potency. I thought, *How strong can the extract of grapefruit seed really be?*

I was about to find out.

Since squirting a few drops in water and stirring it in a cup seemed too time consuming, I just put some directly in my mouth. I swished it around and swallowed. *That was easy*, I thought.

A few moments later, I noticed a rumble of disturbance around my teeth. Soon it felt like an epic battle scene from *Game of Thrones* was taking place inside my mouth. Every inch of my top and bottom gums felt completely on fire. As the heat grew to a distressing intensity, my survival instinct kicked in. *Holy crap, this is really painful!* I thought.

Initially, I just breathed and tried to turn each wave of intensity into a meditation, but the pain was harsh and unrelenting. As it remained at peak intensity, I got up from the couch to look for some form of relief. I splashed cold water on my gums, which only provided momentary relief that then worsened when the burning returned to my awareness. I scoured bathroom drawers for anything that might help and found a tiny bottle of numbing gel for teeth and gums that I had bought months earlier. *Aha!* I thought, *I struck the jackpot!* As my hands literally shook from the pain coursing through such a sensitive part of my body, I was somehow able to apply the gel liberally. Little pieces of cotton from the swab stuck to my gums, but I didn't care. I was hedging my bet on the power of the gel to help me.

Soon, my gums begin to burn *and* tingle. I realized that the gel didn't help at all. It had only added to the fire in my mouth. *This is a complete disaster!* I thought. I grabbed a tissue to wipe the gel and the bits of cotton from my mouth, only to have shreds of tissue now add to the mess. After picking every piece of cotton and tissue out of my gums, I sat on the couch, writhing in pain. First came the thought, *Why is this happening?* Then came the self-blame, *What did I do to deserve this?* Finally, I returned to thinking about how to remedy the situation. So I called a nurse at an urgent care center.

"Sir, I'm sorry," she said quite directly. "There is nothing we can do to help. You're just going to have to ride it out."

As I sat back on the couch in sheer agony, drenched in sweat from head to toe, I just began to laugh. *What an epic dumpster fire of a day! It doesn't matter what I do or don't do; this is what's happening until it changes.* What an unexpected and unprecedented moment of surrender. I laughed even harder as I thought, *I've been afraid of pain most of my life, but always when I was only anticipating it.* As I looked back, I realized that every time I had feared it, I was actually internally free of discomfort. I was unaware of agony's absence because I was too busy anticipating its arrival. Finally I thought, *I can't be afraid of torment and despair. I'm already in it. It's relentless. All I can do is let it guide me on whatever adventure it plans—even when for me, it's an adventure called "This really sucks."*

The intensity took twelve hours to dissipate. It left behind a different version of me—one rooted in a deeper level of bravery who now respects directions printed on little bottles. Without the Universe consulting me beforehand, I became clear on how much I needed an uncompromising dose of pain to help shake off my fixation of trying to avoid it. Instead of fearing its wrath, I respected how it helped me face incredible surges of suffering, even when all avenues of escape had led to dead ends. Somehow, I no longer viewed discomfort as punishment or a barrier to safety. Instead, my safety was determined by how willing I was to survive "what is" no matter how unbearable it was at the time.

This was a moment when my ego experienced how little control it actually had. Once "what is" became my only option, many deeper layers of emotional density began melting away.

The Attribute of Bravery

Through the attribute of bravery, you can move through the discomfort of "what is" without anything to defend, maintain, argue, negotiate, or avoid. As you begin to see how inevitable encounters with pain help you unravel your fear of it, you will be better able to hold unwavering space for yourself and others as you survive dire circumstances.

As your relationship with fear and pain become more heart-centered, your awareness will help you see beyond the categories of like or dislike, which will make facing "what is" more tolerable than you'd ever imagined.

When bravery leads the way, it instinctively provides you with the strength, endurance, grace, and tenacity to overcome the plight of discomfort. Through this attribute, your fear of the unknown will no longer rattle your senses or stifle your ego. Rather, it will help the ego let go of its deeply engrained belief in control. This transforms the realm of the unknown into something curious, intriguing, and even exciting instead of being so overwhelming to process.

In order to go where the ego has never truly gone, it is essential to choose as you've never chosen before. This also means you will more than likely have to feel what you've never felt before—all within a reality of greater support and renewed perspective where you have everything to welcome and nothing to avoid. As you hold greater space during moments of discomfort, you are gathering key pieces of evidence to remind you of how strong, capable, and ready you are to face pain and fear. In gaining more time to notice your true resilience, even when life doesn't offer experiences worth accepting, you'll develop an even greater sense of bravery that will help you rise from the ashes of defeat, devastation, and despair. By cultivating the attribute of bravery, you'll really be present with yourself, while becoming an even stronger source of companionship for the people you choose to support.

From a space-holding perspective, the emotional pain that you must face reflects the visceral intensity of transformation in progress. Whether you're clearing out a deeply lodged layer of emotional debris or witnessing the active expansion of a newly awakening consciousness, the very sensation of discomfort confirms the existential growing pains of your evolving healing journey.

Even when the ego hears this, it can wonder, *Well, is there any way to make it less intense?* While it's natural to wonder this, it's important to recognize that healing occurs as a ratio of time versus intensity. For the journey to be easier, it would require more time. If that happened, though, your ego would become incensed at how slowly life moves along. On the other hand, to be on the most progressive path that offers comprehensive healing, the journey can include reoccurring waves of intensity as your most direct pathway of completion. Since the attribute of bravery helps you overcome the discomfort of "what is," such a high intensity journey can quickly become an exciting opportunity to move beyond each personal limit.

Since the ego often personifies itself as a protector, it is important to remember that it only attempts to shield you from the circumstances and outcomes you continually fear. As you confront each one bravely, you'll find fewer situations to be afraid of, even perhaps discovering how less frightening each moment can be when you face "what is" instead of imagining "what if." Such a definitive shift ultimately leaves your ego with no one to coddle, convince, or control. This causes the ego to meet the inevitability of its own demise, unaware that what it perceives as death is actually a doorway to eternal rebirth. Through the attribute of bravery, your ability to hold space compassionately releases the ego from its belief in control, which allows such a profound moment of letting go to occur.

As I wrote in *The Universe Always Has a Plan*, "You are not the one who lets go. You are the one being let go of." This means that while many people attempt to let go as if it's a willful process, it is actually a rather spontaneous unfolding of being released from the ego's grip, once it sees control as nothing more than an idea it once believed in.

Ironically, the ego, which is the only part of you in a constant battle against the threat of "what is," doesn't actually know what it's fighting or avoiding beyond its belief in frightening ideas. While the nature of each circumstance highlights uninterruptible milestones of healing, you do possess the power to determine how insightful or intolerable any moment can be. Through the attribute of bravery, you no longer wait for a perfect sign from the Universe to face what's already happening or meant to occur. Instead, your ability to hold space helps you enter the next highest level in your journey even when it presents itself as the very situation you had hoped to avoid.

What Could Possibly Go Wrong?

When facing "what is," all too often, whatever the ego can't control represents what we believe could possibly go wrong. In fact, just because the ego thinks a situation has gone awry doesn't mean you've made a mistake or engaged in any wrongdoing. Beyond moments of abuse (which always require swift action in the name of your sovereignty and safety), we commonly perceive unfairness from others when the ego doesn't get its way. As another form of irony, even if the ego constantly got its way, it would be no happier than before.

Since the ego commonly perceives pain as a barrier to happiness, it insists that only in pain's absence can true happiness exist. In truth, happiness is an extension of aliveness. Aliveness is the will to live. The more you say yes to living on life's unpredictable terms, the more happiness you may experience. While it's beyond the ego's capacity to imagine how happiness and pain can coexist in the same field of reality, it's never beyond your awareness to appreciate how freeing painful experiences can be, even when they show up as unwelcomed moments of intensity.

From the ego's perspective, the question of what could possibly go wrong also includes the triggering of deep vulnerabilities since it sees feelings of sensitivity as a weakness that increases the threat of rejection. In reality, the more you are stripped of your defenses and rendered helpless by the hands of fate, the greater the likelihood of establishing intimate connections. Perhaps the ego considers vulnerability a weakness because it has no access to the attribute of bravery that makes it a gift instead of a curse. This is why you are such a vital part of your healing journey, not only as the one who experiences evolutionary change but as the space holder who has access to the very bravery that allows facing "what is" to unfold with grace.

When not getting your way is no longer proof of bad luck, a karmic setback, evidence of a low vibration, or any other kind of judgment, you will leap across the threshold of victimhood into a renewed depth of empowerment. While the ego believes, *I'd be much more open, if only things were different*, it is the attribute of bravery that reminds you that there will never be a better time to lean into pain or face discomfort than at the moment it begins. Whether such experiences bring out the worst in others, lead to fights among family members in crisis, widen a wedge of discord in relationships, or even create unexpected loss—you can face each circumstance with your highest values and deepest strengths intact when fueled by the power of your own unwavering support.

All that is required is a willingness to be brave, even while holding space for the aspects of self that know of no other way but to be afraid.

It is also important to remember that there is no wrong way to be brave. There are simply moments of courageous resolve that may not go as planned. Isn't that okay? Isn't it okay, even when a strong response of dislike makes unwelcomed change seem like something that shouldn't be happening. Isn't it okay that the ego can think, imagine, or conclude anything it wants without preventing you from taking the very steps that only seem scary the more you delay the inevitable?

Imagine holding a frightened child in your arms who says, "I'm too scared to keep going." Through the attribute of bravery you can say, "I really know how you feel, but we can only find true safety in moving forward."

While many people insist they aren't brave enough to face looming hardships, frustrations, or discomforts, it is the facing of these uncomfortable experiences, no matter how fearful we may be, that brings our deepest bravery to life.

Setting an Intention for Bravery

To release any fear of pain and patterns of avoidance and hold a space of bravery for yourself and others, please repeat the following words out loud:

I intend to hold space through the attribute of bravery for myself and others, no matter how uncomfortable, inconvenient, or frustrating it seems to be. I allow bravery to be offered in honor of my integrating ego that cannot prevent me from facing "what is" with the control it only imagines having. Whether my ego thinks it has control, gets its way, or fights for something to defend or maintain, I allow the wisdom of courage to always reveal my next evolutionary step forward. By embracing the attribute of bravery, I allow the fear of pain and patterns of avoidance to be cleared from my energy field, returned to the Source of its origin, transmuted completely, and healed to completion now.

In knowing it is so, I allow the attribute of bravery to infuse a renewed strength of divinity within me to be expressed from a willingness to be vulnerable, no matter how it's received, overlooked, or denied, or whether I agree with the viewpoints of any personal sharing. If and when this hurts my feelings, triggers memories of past traumas, makes me more distrusting of others, causes me to shut down in rejection or lash out in resentment, or instigates palpable signs of exhaustion, I allow myself the sacred space to be with my feelings and offer the gift of bravery to any frightened part of me. Whether given to myself or another person or as an active blessing to humanity, I allow the attribute of bravery to transform scared into sacred by rearranging the way I view each moment from a space-holding perspective. And so it is.

The Supportive Statement of Bravery

"No Matter How You Feel, You Can Do This"

While your gift of support can make someone's excruciating pain easier to bear, it is common for their ego to look to you as a new potential hiding spot. When that person is actively in a state of avoidance, their ego will likely use anything to stall for more time, unaware that the more it avoids, the scarier the facing of pain will feel. This can lead to bargaining for a different experience, begging you to help them escape what they're afraid to confront, engaging in compulsive behavior such as various forms of addiction, and even sudden bursts of cruelty. This is why, in order to be an empowered space holder and not an enabler of avoidance, the supportive statement of bravery is "No matter how you feel, you can do this."

Through these words, you remind someone how ready they are to venture into unknown territory or even confront their deepest fears only to come out on the other side—renewed and reborn. It is always important to remember that you're not trying to convince them that they can do what they insist they can't. When you have no attachment to outcome, just by letting them know "No matter how you feel, you can do this," your gift of space holding allows them to remember the bravery that's always inside them.

This supportive statement acts as a catalyst to bravery, simply because your belief in a person's capabilities, even when they hide in isolation or trust others more than themselves, surely helps them feel a greater sense of community. Through the encouragement of others, the truth of unity consciousness helps each human being accomplish what they may have thought they could never achieve on their own. Whether you feel someone's greater capacity of strength or merely hope they find such capabilities within themselves, the gift of belief that you instill in another provides an opportunity for their consciousness to operate from a more grounded, focused, and assertive position. Since adversities can feel like life is tearing everything down around them, the importance of bravery's wisdom helps build the confidence necessary for them to do what they may have never done before.

Even when your supportive statement leads someone to shut down, refuse to try, or run away, your ability to bravely believe in another's greatness cultivates an equal belief in yourself. Perhaps the bravery you seek comes from declaring out loud the suggestion, "No matter how I feel, I can do this." Just by repeating these words of empowerment, you remind yourself of all you can face and overcome, regardless of how you feel about it. While many people confuse the apprehension of ego with an intuitive sign to turn away and run in the opposite direction, the bravery you embody politely removes these misinterpretations of intuitive guidance from the ego's grip. Whether hope feels surprisingly within reach or millions of miles away, the most unexpected blessings can arrive at the doorstep of your experience just by daring to remember "No matter how you feel, you can do this."

Bravery in Action

Through the attribute of bravery, you are more likely to step out of your comfort zone to discover how different life can be when it no longer exists as an object the ego manages, protects, or controls.

Perhaps you need to have a rather difficult conversation with a friend, coworker, or relative in need in which your deep, unshakeable desire to reach out to them outweighs the threat of being disliked. Can you go where you may not want to go, simply so you know in the depths of your heart that you did everything in your power to support the health, well-being, and happiness of another?

Instead of believing the pain you are in or the losses you've endured are forms of karmic punishment, what if they became opportunities to stop hiding in patterns of self-blame? Are you ready to make peace with the mystery of life that always gets its way solely for the advancement of your highest evolutionary benefit?

Maybe it's not the people in your life who exhaust you but the deeper truths you are afraid to share that cause you to feel so drained?

What if by avoiding discomfort, you preserve the ego's best hiding spot? What if avoidance only creates greater separation from the true autonomy, fulfillment, liberation, and joy you desire and deserve?

Perhaps the sensation of fear is only a sign of something to avoid when the conditioning of ego interprets it. The question remains: Are you the preserver of such unbearable patterning or its faithfully brave liberator?

Bravery as a Daily Practice

To bring the attribute of bravery to the forefront of your awareness, try one or all of these daily practices:

- Make a list of the most intimidating or overwhelming action steps you continually put off or avoid. From a renewed space of bravery and empowerment, may you dare to accomplish each task, at whatever pace is most supportive to your experience, leaving you nothing to fear, overthink, or deny. May you view each item as the perfect opportunity to remind yourself, "No matter how you feel, you can do this."

- Make a point to send at least one text message a day to someone in your contact list, telling them, "I believe in you." Even if you've done this as a daily practice from earlier chapters with people in your closest inner circle, take the next step by sending this text to someone who you lost contact with or haven't spoken to in a while. You can also say this during fleeting interactions with neighbors. Or write it on the bill as an inspirational message to your restaurant server.

- If you hear about a tragedy, may you be willing to focus more on those who are surviving the unthinkable than enduring the pain of hardship as a way to further expand the attribute of bravery within yourself.

CHAPTER 10

Time Is the
Wisest Healer

Since moving out of California to pursue my career as a healer, I began seeing my parents in a different light. The more I held space for the feelings I had gathered and suppressed, the more easily I could view my entire family as many souls on an incredible journey together. Instead of fixating on the disappointments, moments of betrayal, and even the confusion of not knowing which version of my parents stood before me, I now saw two people who had found love together and who were always my biggest fans—no matter how many stumbles it took for me to find my way.

As I matured in adulthood, I began to viscerally sense how much pressure they both lived with. My dad worked in sales every day of his life to spite the parents he felt had judged him, while my mom carried the weight of the world on her shoulders as a parent, paralegal, PTA president, and power of attorney for my grandfather. With time came tremendous perspective. I began to wonder if they could have ever satisfied my childhood desires, even if every incident of confusion or difficulty had been different. What if, as an innocent consequence of being a kid, I would have always perceived them to be inadequate in some form or fashion? It's not as if they didn't behave the way they did, but with time as the wisest healer, I was able to feel more into their experience than remaining attached to mine.

Eventually, I understood why two of the smartest people I'd ever known couldn't perceive what I saw so clearly. The answer was simple. I was a witness outside of them. I had a fresh, open perspective that was free of the stresses and pressures they regularly lived out.

Such a realization came five years before my father's passing. As it dropped in from the heavens, the voice of my intuition was so loud and clear. It said, *Within a few years, both of your parents will pass.* I was in the shower at the time, and out of nowhere, the reality that I would have to say goodbye to both of them struck me profoundly. I wailed so deeply, huge silent pauses swelled in between each wave of tears. I remember declaring out loud, "I'm so sorry Mom and Dad. You did the best you could, and it was more than enough. You gave me an incredible life filled with love and support, no matter how it felt in my sensitive body. Please forgive me for ever judging you. May the next few years be the best our relationship could ever be."

From that fateful moment, I began relating to my parents with more understanding, even though they hadn't changed at all. I even shared with them the words I'd declared in the shower. It was a moment of true existential relief to watch their eyes fill with admiration for how grateful I was for my perfectly imperfect upbringing. Although my childhood was rather intense for my empathic sensitivities, it was also exactly what I needed to prepare me for the healing work I was here to complete in myself and offer to others.

As they hugged me and said, "There is nothing to forgive Matthew. We are the ones who are sorry," I felt deeply buried layers of familial patterning such as shame and guilt lift out of us. It was a moment of sweet victory. We were souls dressed up as people playing out all we intended to resolve together. In that moment, it was as if my mom, dad, and I removed the masks of our characters to congratulate each other as cosmic companions who had made it to a stage of transformation we had on some level agreed to help each other reach.

Just as my intuition had stated, a few years later, both of my parents began experiencing a steady decline in health. My dad deteriorated quickly. One day he wasn't feeling well, and it seemed as if the next, he was in a hospice bed in my childhood home clinging to each breath. At this point, my mom's cancer, rheumatoid arthritis, and Raynaud's syndrome had taken the use of her fingers and her ability to walk without assistance. For a woman who always needed something to control, this was devastating. She sat in a wheelchair beside my father with no ability to reach over and touch him as he died. We moved my mom's hand onto his, so she could be with him during his final moments.

"I love you, Herb," she sobbed to the only man she had ever loved. "I'm so sorry for any pain I caused you. You were the best husband and father. I'm going to miss you." I rubbed my mom's back while I felt the agony of her breaking heart as the mask of her ego shattered. As a child, I'd always fantasized about the day my parents would realize the gravity of their shortcomings, and here it was right in front of me. Was this my long-awaited moment of redemption? Absolutely not. In watching my mother's control patterns explode into chaos as she sat beside her dying husband—while feeling miles away from him due to a body she couldn't really maneuver—my heart broke with hers.

Witnessing the implosion of my mom's control pattern as her inner child's helplessness peeked out from behind the walls of anger and sarcasm it had hidden behind rattled me to my core and changed me for the better. It would be the exact moment I truly knew what it meant to forgive. In seeing firsthand how much pain my mom's wounds had caused her, I realized she had also been a victim in her own life. She wasn't against me, my sister, or my dad, nor was my dad against me, my sister, or my mom. We were all on the same side, each having been hurt by the patterns of unprocessed pain that we came to Earth to resolve.

The last two years of my mom's life without my dad were brutal. Instead of her control patterns dissolving completely, they amped up in many ways. But after seeing how my dad's death had left her emotionally gutted, I now regarded her behavior through a lens of unwavering compassion. Her antics used to bother me at nearly every turn, but that was when I was only viewing them from the perspective of my own pain. Once I recognized how much conflict she was in and how deeply it was buried within her, literally nothing she could have said or done would have upset me.

This clarity also helped me realize that once you become aware of how much suffering a person carries, forgiveness is an instinct that comes over you, not a choice you need to make. Years before, in the shower, I had chosen to forgive. While it felt relieving on a superficial level, the true forgiveness I offered silently at my dad's deathbed was an instinctive response to witnessing my mom's despair as directly as I had known my own. Once I recognized that my mom and I were two people in pain, there was nothing for me to feel but forgiveness.

During my mom's passing, I could sense my dad's spirit along with some of her deceased relatives and spirit guides standing in a doorway of light ready to welcome her home. My sister and I both wanted her to be with my dad and free from the physical complications that had ravaged her body so mercilessly. As she took her final breath, I felt a wave of existential relief wash over me. The contract we had signed to play out as mom, dad, and son was now complete. It's one thing to hear about soul contracts as a concept, but it's an entirely different experience when you discover a knowing so viscerally.

Once I recognized how the pain of carrying a lifetime of hurt was equal to the pain the person who hurt me carried throughout their lifetime, the attribute of forgiveness came alive within me. Far beyond the judgments of like or dislike, there is no way to explain the humility, harmony, and mercy that flowed inside me when I witnessed how much pain my mother had buried within herself.

Instead of fighting how you feel or working to escape the memories still swirling in your mind, you too may find yourself unexpectedly supporting the salvation of your most notorious assailant by asking that they be forgiven—no matter what role they played. Not because what happened was justifiable by any means but to break the cycle of abuse, neglect, and trauma that fills each heart with the despair of human suffering.

The Attribute of Forgiveness

Through the attribute of forgiveness, you allow any grudge, hatred, or judgment toward someone who hurt you to dissolve as you become more aware of the pain they carry. While the ego will act as your protector by ridiculing their shortcomings and condemning hurtful behavior, with time as the wisest healer, you'll find your own journey coming to a place of resolution as you sense the unbearable pain they once hid in you. Even if you're the one who harmed another, as you become more acutely aware of your own unprocessed pain, you will grow to be more merciful toward yourself as you face the darker parts most people deny.

Contrary to the ego's belief, forgiveness is not about justifying intolerable behavior, turning blame onto the victim, becoming someone's punching bag, rationalizing the pain you've endured, or even using spiritual concepts like "soul contracts" to stay in toxic partnership. It's more the case of realizing your pain is equal to the torment lurking in people who acted out of character in horrific, self-serving, or damaging ways.

Before forgiveness dawns authentically, the ego can use your history of pain to develop an identity of righteous entitlement. It so commonly believes, *Because I was the one who endured unfair treatment, I have the right to treat those who hurt me any way I wish until I've decided they've had enough*. While the ego fantasizes about the day each attacker is rendered helpless, has surrendered, and begs for mercy, the moment you see the infinite skeletons stuck inside the closet of another person's heart, you will discover a level of forgiveness that is beyond the realm of choice and rational comprehension. This experience can't be rushed, rehearsed, or anticipated, which is why time is the wisest healer—always helping to prepare you for this life-changing revelation.

As you read these words, it's common for the ego to think, *Even if I saw how much pain they carry, I would still never forgive them*. This is actually true, since the ego tries to obtain control by being in charge of forgiving. But the ego itself is not the one who forgives. Rather, it's the immaculate grace of the Universe forgiving someone on your behalf as a new level of consciousness expands within you. In waking up to sense the oneness within and throughout all people, any wounds of discord that linger between hearts will be spontaneously released. With the attribute of forgiveness being the compassionate force through which the truth of oneness emerges in all of us, your willingness to notice the severity of pain in those who hurt you helps inspire this act of grace. This is true even when the pain is so deeply buried in one of your assailants, they seem to be a person who has it together and somehow got away with hurting others.

Since you're always being prepared for such a spontaneous moment of forgiveness, when it occurs, it is always a milestone of expansion that happens through you, rather than by you.

Do you know why many people can't offer forgiveness? It's because they themselves are not in charge of when and how it unfolds. Until such an immaculate shift in perspective occurs, it is essential to equally hold space for the healing of your own suffering, while slowly but surely opening to the fact that all the pain you find in yourself is the same imprinting of pain that others who hurt you carry in their bodies. May this insight also bring to an end the victim shaming that occurs when someone who still has pain to process is made to feel inadequate for being unable to forgive.

Even with these two interconnected points in focus, the ego is quick to say, *So what?! They have pain. Who cares? What about me?* Thankfully, this belief can't create a barrier to healing since the goal is not coaxing forgiveness from the ego in any way. Instead you will hear such repetitive, self-indulgent thoughts that they inspire a sudden wake-up call that escorts you out of the character you've played in your family, relationships, and work environments. As your awareness expands beyond the framework of your ego's identity, you will have no sense of who deserves healing more than anyone else. Instead the embodied grace of space holding will reveal to you a depth of healing that has no bias or agenda other than shining the light of oneness for the mutual liberation of all.

Through the attribute of forgiveness, it is not a matter of trying to be forgiving as a way of fast-tracking healing relief. Rather, you become so objectively aware of pain that it opens up the remembrance that everyone deserves to be liberated from the plight of human suffering. While the ego may dream of vengeance and retribution toward those it felt it was wronged, neglected, or abused by, it becomes impossible to maintain such an adversarial attitude when you are able to acknowledge the prison of despair most people live in and react from. Even when those who hurt you have been swiftly brought to justice and kept from hurting others by serving a life sentence, no matter how deeply the ego insists, you can't deny the unexplainable resolve that washes over you when true forgiveness arrives.

OPENING GREATER SPACE FOR TRUE FORGIVENESS TO BLOSSOM

Imagine you are in Heaven and that you receive a message that Source wants to speak with you. With excitement in your heart, you wonder, *What could this be?*

Within a second, you are in the direct presence of Source energy who says, "I have a mission for you. Are you willing to be guided?"

"Yes, of course, I am!" you say with delight, before asking, "What's the mission you have in mind?"

"I created an Earth plane to manifest the unending light of all into materialized form, so Heaven may know itself as tangible physical matter," Source replies. "Each inhabitant that dwells on Earth is an opportunity for Heaven to know itself in every combination of individuality. Heaven has gotten to know itself in many ways through Earth's evolution, but in order to know itself in a unique way it never has before, you have been chosen to incarnate as Heaven's next level of embodied realization."

"I'm so honored. What do I need to know before incarnating?" you ask.

"Your agreement sets every facet of your existence into motion—from start to finish. Anything you will need to know will be provided to you through the unfolding of each experience. Not to worry. If you overlook instructions, they will repeat until you see and receive them. Your success is guaranteed with the freedom to experience each moment however you desire to view it."

With your blissful nod of agreement, Source furthers your mission. "While you may forget these words initially, please heed these instructions. You will gradually remember them as you awaken. You will evolve from one spectrum of consciousness to the next, both gathering experiences and encountering characters, solely for the purpose of Heaven's evolution through you. Heaven's mission is to cultivate its highest attributes in physical form through your unique expression. If there is pain, it's only furthering a journey that leads to joy. If there is abandonment, it's only to lead you in the direction of greater inclusion. If there is sadness, it's only as a means of deepening Heaven's knowing of happiness. If there is suffering, it's only to shape perspectives, so an awareness of liberation may dawn.

"Other characters will be placed in your path to help you deepen, refine, and master each essential attribute, knowing how any degree of low only sets the stage to discover the next greatest high, no matter how often you move back and forth. All the while, it will be Heaven's unique exploration to know itself as you, while you remember the Heaven that has always dwelled within. No matter which character you encounter, how despicably they act, or how separate the Earth realm feels from your Heavenly home, please know, it is I who dwell in all characters, including you, as a silent reminder that only the hands of Source are shaping your highest form of mastery and guiding you along—from one experience to the next."

As you process these instructions, a sensation strikes you, almost like a feeling of vanishing. The next thing you know, you are looking through the lens of a camera with tiny legs kicking out in front of you as unfamiliar faces gather around to marvel at their newly born family member. This is when Heaven's journey of knowing thyself has begun. It's the very moment the attribute of forgiveness starts to grow while nurtured by time as the greatest healer of all.

What Could Possibly Go Wrong?

Since the dawning of true forgiveness is beyond your will or control, the only thing that can go wrong is trying to forgive before it happens authentically on its own. While it's natural to desire freedom from pain and suffering, you can't force the power of forgiveness by uttering the three-word phrase "I forgive you."

When you understand that you can't coerce yourself to forgive, it's equally true that you can't move someone else closer to it, no matter how much more connected you would feel if only the other person could "get there" faster.

Since the effects of forgiveness are spontaneous, it begs the question, What is being cultivated in the attribute of forgiveness? It's a quality of becoming forgiving. This doesn't put you in charge of forgiveness but simply softens each inner edge by helping you become more aware of the pain that exists in those who hurt you. This means that a greater awareness of your own suffering deepens your ability to hold space for the pain, fear, and judgment existing in others. From this space, you are preparing for the auspicious moment when true forgiveness dawns. Until that point, it's not a matter of rushing the process or helpful for anyone to suggest that you should forgive, when in fact, it's one of the most incredible gifts each person is destined to spontaneously receive.

Even when you notice the indignant refusal to forgive yourself, instead of feeling bad or thinking you're failing your healing journey, why not use this as an opportunity to thank each painful part within you for staying true to itself and the path it's on?

While the ego believes, *If only I could heal everything at record speed, then I'd have more time for the things I want and less time for the things I don't want,* the truth is, each milestone of experience was created with flawless intention prior to your birth. Free will comes into play in how you choose to see any particular moment. With time on your side, the sacred art of space holding releases you from the tendency to micro-manage your journey or control someone else's evolution. Instead, the pace of transformation is slowed, so as to come into more authentic communion with yourself, your loved ones, those you know, and even those you may ignore or despise.

Whether your life is currently playing out as moments of existential release, emotional hardship, debilitating pain, profound exhaustion, or spontaneous bursts of merciful grace, you can cherish each gain and loss for how beautifully it was orchestrated for the evolutionary benefit of all who enter the atmosphere of this magical planet. Without needing to rush the process, shame a victim, or imagine all you are missing by being exactly where you're meant to be, why not take a deep breath and congratulate yourself on how far you've come, while knowing in the depths of your heart—no matter what has happened, everything is made right in the end.

Setting an Intention for Forgiveness

To soften each edge and hold a space of forgiveness for yourself and others, please repeat the following words out loud:

I intend to hold space through the attribute of forgiveness for myself and others, no matter the pain I feel or the grudges I hold. I allow the attribute of forgiveness to be cultivated as a way of softening each edge by embracing time as the wisest healer of all. No matter how often my ego tries to be in charge of forgiveness, I accept it's a process that cannot be coerced, manipulated, or fast-tracked. This may help me understand the attribute of forgiveness as the process of softening the edges of my heart by becoming aware of how the pain living in me equally dwells in those who have hurt me. By embracing the attribute of forgiveness as an entry point into the truth of oneness, I allow all beliefs in duality, separation from Source, falling from grace, and patterns of comparison, competition, and discord to be cleared out of my energy field, returned to the Source of its origin, transmuted completely, and healed to completion now.

In knowing it is so, I allow the attribute of forgiveness to inspire my deepest heartfelt surrender, no matter how it's received, overlooked, or denied, or whether I agree with the viewpoints of any personal sharing. If and when this hurts my feelings, triggers memories of past traumas, makes me more distrusting of others, causes me to shut down in rejection or lash out in resentment, or instigates palpable signs of exhaustion, I allow myself the sacred space to be with my feelings and offer the gift of my forgiving nature to any broken part of me. Whether given to myself or another person or as an active blessing to humanity, I welcome and allow the attribute of forgiveness as my contribution toward the healing of all. And so it is.

The Supportive Statement of Forgiveness

"No Matter What Has Happened, Everything Is Made Right in the End"

Through the attribute of forgiveness, you embrace the dimension of time as the wisest healer of all. While the ego believes that you will heal at the speed you get things "right," the unwavering beauty of time gently guides you along, always preparing you for outcomes and circumstances you don't have to anticipate in any way. You may think, *But if I were more prepared, I'd be able to go through each moment with fewer emotions being triggered.* Yet, when you are emotionally triggered, it confirms how this moment was created for exactly the amount of healing you are now ready to process. This is why the supportive statement of forgiveness is "No matter what has happened, everything is made right in the end."

Without having to figure out how to forgive, your role as a sacred space holder is to know in your heart that everything is made right and whole by a loving creator that only knows perfection as the nature of reality. When leading with the forgiving words "No matter what has happened, everything is made right in the end," you allow everyone the right to their process, regardless of how slowly it evolves or how often patterns repeat.

This statement also acts as a validator of pain, a reminder that wholeness always has the final say, and a promise that destiny continues to work tirelessly on your behalf to remind you of Heaven continually knowing itself through your unique evolution. As you dare to be softer than the edges you sense in others, more open-minded than the judgments you imagine, and more aligned with the dimension of time than the unconscious fast pace of modern society, you will have settled into the optimal perspective as a sacred space holder aligned with the holiest truth of oneness in all. Whether this is already awake within you, continuing to open over time, or about to ignite a spark of divinity unlike anything you've ever experienced, it only masquerades as an ever-changing world to ensure for each individual "No matter what has happened, everything is made right in the end."

Forgiveness in Action

Through the attribute of forgiveness, your awareness of human suffering becomes the ultimate equalizer helping you unravel patterns of righteous entitlement often created by echoes of repressed pain.

Perhaps instead of judging the cruelty of others, you will find a moment of reflection, imagining how much they must have endured to treat themselves or another human being so poorly. While this perspective of empathy doesn't justify anyone's inhumane behavior, it reminds you that a world free of suffering can't occur with perpetual shaming, damaging gossip, or righteous forms of condemnation. While some predators require prison sentences in order to spare the innocence of others, the swiftness of justice coupled with the merciful awareness of other people's pain can always coexist in exactly the same space.

Maybe you have shamed yourself for being unable to forgive. Can this be the moment you reach out to your most hurtful parts with the love, presence, and compassion of true heartfelt acceptance?

What if how much time it takes to heal or is spent "wanting" versus "having" is not a matter of getting better at manifesting what you desire but an opportunity to see how your life has been orchestrated to inspire the very layers of repressed emotion you were born to heal? What if you are the reason every gift is given but are never to blame for why what you want has yet to arrive? Are you ready to honor time as the greatest healer, instead of viewing it as a barrier to the joy always within you?

Maybe from this renewed space-holding perspective, it's okay that everything is exactly the way it is. Maybe it's okay that people hold grudges until they don't. Maybe it's okay that everything happened exactly as it did. Maybe it's even okay that nothing has to be okay for any reason. Maybe it's okay to be not okay and to notice how the beauty of evolution still unfolds with perfection—no matter what you like or dislike along the way?

Perhaps since "no matter what has happened, everything is made right in the end," you don't have to work so hard at figuring everything out. Instead, you can simply be the receiver of evolutionary grace, letting everything that is meant to happen occur within its own unique time frame. Even when the ego thinks evolution needs to move faster, you can simply place your hand on your heart and give yourself the gift of compassionate support in response to any frustration.

Forgiveness as a Daily Practice

To bring the attribute of forgiveness to the forefront of your awareness, try one or all of these daily practices:

- For each person who disturbs, angers, or frustrates you, take a moment to contemplate how much loss, suffering, trauma, and despair they must have endured to be who they are. May each time you become lost in blame inspire a contemplation of their suffering to set each judgment free.

- Meditation is a process of making peace with time. When you find a momentary pause to savor each inhale and exhale, you cultivate harmony that allows even greater space for the truth of oneness to emerge. While meditation can't force an awakening to occur, it sends a message of readiness that allows the miracles, magic, and synchronicity of Universal Will to enter the domain of your awareness.

- If you find yourself out of harmony with the dimension of time, try declaring one of life's timeless truths: *I may or may not always get what I want, but I always have everything I need.* May you feel how such wisdom gently slows the nervous system and grounds you back into the present moment. For greater expansion, try slowly repeating this declaration five to ten times, as often throughout the day as need be.

Conclusion

Through this journey of holding space, you have learned how listening is the first step to being helpful. When you remember that it's not a matter of what you or someone else *doesn't* know and that you can't rush what has been buried for so long, the beauty of intimate connection can flourish exquisitely. When anger is a reenactment of someone's trauma, it's likely to reveal a person fighting their pain, especially whenever you get pushed away. This can renew the depth of your compassion, so you don't overly personalize their despair as another wound for you to process. As diversity becomes the guiding light of compassion, you are better able to honor boundaries as acts of self-love. From this space of greater heartfelt connection, you will have cultivated a true sense of emotional balance to help you honor your own needs and support the journey of others without overgiving from states of exhaustion. Since gratitude is always appropriate, when magnified in your awareness, you're likely to sense the all-inclusive presence of divinity whether confronted by something you personally like or dislike. While facing "what is" can be uncomfortable, and that's okay, it's a gift of liberation, freeing you from fear while slowing you down to recognize time as the wisest healer of all.

Whether for yourself or in response to another, may you listen with encouragement, lead with validation, share perspectives of reverence, respond with mercy, embody worthiness, embrace patience, demonstrate respect, show appreciation, live with bravery, and allow forgiveness to awaken for the healing, liberation, and well-being of our beloved planet.

May holding space be an inner declaration and ongoing prayer that you bring with you in direct response to the details and demands of your ever-changing world. Since holding space is a gift of empowerment you can openly share, I invite the capacity of your greatest effort and the majestic wonder of your innate courage to begin leading the way on your behalf.

May it bring to you the living adventure you have been seeking.

May it answer the questions lingering in your mind.

May it show you the way across a threshold of despair and into a paradise of compassionate resolve.

May it absolve you of wounding, make peace with your past, and set into motion a voyage home into the infinite depths of your divine heart space.

From this moment forward, may the destiny of your awakened heart shine freely for the benefit of all who enter your immaculate presence. Through the transformative power of holding space, this is what it means to live All for Love. Whether this is our first time meeting or a connection deepening between group healing events, it has been a true honor to serve your evolution throughout each page and have you as a part of mine. Thank you for this gift.

ACKNOWLEDGMENTS

First and foremost, I would like to thank you, the reader, for opening your heart to this new way of heart-centered engagement and inviting each gift I was born to share into your life. May they serve you well along your ever-expanding path of self-love and integrated embodiment.

I would like to thank my sister, Shannon, and my remaining family for their continued support, including my parents who both reside in Heaven and watch over me. Thank you Mom and Dad for your regular visits, and your permission to share the personal stories that help make the holding space process a compelling life-changing journey for all who embrace it. And thank you for your unwavering support and belief in me and your enthusiasm to have me share our memories and life lessons that bring such invaluable healing to relationships and families worldwide.

I would also like to thank my team for their daily support and acts of loving service in helping me to further and fulfill my life's mission. Whether you've been with me during pivotal stages throughout my expansion or have been with me since the very beginning, I thank you from the bottom of my heart for all of your help and devotion as we serve the awakening of humanity.

Thank you to my literary agent and dear friend, Kenny Wapner, for being an amazing guiding light throughout this entire process.

A special thank-you to Tami Simon, Jaime Schwalb, and everyone at Sounds True for being an absolute joy to work with on every level. As Dorothy said at the end of *The Wizard of Oz*,

"There's no place like home." Another special thank-you to Susan Golant for being an impeccable editorial wizard whom I am so blessed to always learn from.

Finally, I would like to thank my divine guidance for the transmissions of energy infused in each written and spoken word, along with every member of the Love Revolution, who have come together as one for the benefit of our awakening planet.

I love you all from the depths of my soul. As I always say, this isn't the end. It's only the beginning of a brand-new adventure.

All for love,
Matt Kahn

ABOUT THE AUTHOR

Matt Kahn is the author of the bestselling books *Whatever Arises, Love That*, *Everything Is Here to Help You*, and *The Universe Always Has a Plan*. He is a spiritual teacher and highly attuned empathic healer who serves the awakening and evolution of all sentient beings through his heart-centered offerings. His global audience is finding the support they seek to feel more loved, awakened, and empowered to the greatest possibilities in life during this critical time in history.

Matt's spontaneous awakening arose from of an out-of-body experience in early childhood, and through his direct experiences with Ascended Masters and archangels throughout his life. Using his intuitive abilities of seeing, hearing, feeling, and direct knowing, Matt brings forth revolutionary teachings through both the written and spoken word that assist energetically sensitive beings in healing the body, awakening the soul, and transforming reality through the power of love.

ABOUT SOUNDS TRUE

Sounds True is a multimedia publisher whose mission is to inspire and support personal transformation and spiritual awakening. Founded in 1985 and located in Boulder, Colorado, we work with many of the leading spiritual teachers, thinkers, healers, and visionary artists of our time. We strive with every title to preserve the essential "living wisdom" of the author or artist. It is our goal to create products that not only provide information to a reader or listener but also embody the quality of a wisdom transmission.

For those seeking genuine transformation, Sounds True is your trusted partner. At SoundsTrue.com you will find a wealth of free resources to support your journey, including exclusive weekly audio interviews, free downloads, interactive learning tools, and other special savings on all our titles.

To learn more, please visit SoundsTrue.com/freegifts or call us toll-free at 800.333.9185.

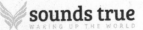

I Love You